COOL CAREERS WITHOUT COLLEGE FOR

PEOPLE WHO LOVE TO BUY THINGS

COOL CAREERS WITHOUT COLLEGE FOR
PEOPLE
WHO LOVE
TO BUY
THINGS

**EDSON
SANTOS**

The Rosen Publishing Group, Inc., New York

To A.L.S.—who's so much fun to shop with...

Published in 2007 by The Rosen Publishing Group, Inc.
29 East 21st Street, New York, NY 10010

Library of Congress Cataloging-in-Publication Data

MHS apple $33.25 4·07

Santos, Edson.
Cool careers without college for people who love to buy things/
Edson Santos.
     p. cm.—(Cool careers without college)
Includes index.
ISBN 1-4042-0751-1 (library binding)
1. Purchasing—Vocational guidance—Juvenile literature.
2. Purchasing agents—Juvenile literature. I. Title. II. Series.

HF5437.S26 2006
658.7'2023-dc22

                                        2005034075

Manufactured in the United States of America

CONTENTS

INTRODUCTION

Shopping is a favorite pastime in the United States and Canada. However, buying things can be much more than a leisure activity, a chore, an obsession, or a form of therapy; it can also be a challenging, exciting, and profitable way to make a living.

In North America, where the consumer is king (or queen), buying is one of the most common yet complex activities. As you know, everything under the sun can be bought and sold. However, purchasing intelligently—knowing how to track down high-quality merchandise for the best possible price—is an art that requires skill and expertise. As this book will show, you can make a good living buying clothes, shares in different companies, antiques, movie props, Christmas presents, or vacation homes. In most cases, you don't need a college degree to be a good purchaser. The keys to success are being a thorough researcher, communicator, and negotiator; knowing your products, suppliers, and customers; and having a passion for deal making. Also essential is having an instinct or flair for shopping—for finding the perfect item that will satisfy your clients' needs and desires.

Although professional shoppers, buyers, and purchasers don't get to keep the things they buy, they do get to enjoy the thrill of the hunt without having to fork out their own money. The satisfaction of buying someone the ideal birthday present; finding the perfect knife for a film's crucial murder scene; closing on a couple's first house; or buying work from a starving artist for an influential art collector's home are often rewards in themselves. Frequently, the purchases you make, or help make, not only bring people happiness but also improve their lives. Ultimately, purchasing can positively affect people's lives, as well as the welfare of companies, industries, and even an entire nation's economy.

The twelve occupations described in this book offer a sampling of the diverse buying careers that exist. Some, such as antique dealer, stockbroker, and real estate agent, are classic professions that have been around for a long time. Others, such as personal shopper, wardrobe stylist, and mystery shopper, are less obvious occupations that promise opportunities in keeping with our increasingly sophisticated economies and societies.

1

PROP BUYER

Have you ever been on a treasure hunt? Did you like using clues to find a specific item and racing to track it down before anybody else? Many professional prop buyers compare their jobs to being on a treasure hunt. Prop buyers locate frequently hard-to-find, unusual objects to be used for films, plays, TV shows, advertisements, and magazine layouts. If the notion of hunting treasure for a living appeals to you, you might want to look into becoming a prop buyer.

Job Description

Props are portable objects used to decorate a film or stage set or used by actors in a movie, play, or television program. A set of Victorian china, a potted orchid, a unicycle, a goldfish in a bowl, a cell phone, a gun—all of these are props. Depending on a director's needs and vision, and the prop budget, props will either be constructed or purchased. In the latter case, the prop manager, who oversees all props, will hire a prop buyer to track down and buy or rent the items needed.

Buying props often entails a great deal of research and footwork. Prop rental shops and Web sites (such as eBay.com) abound. Some specialize in exotic items such as medieval armor, monster and horror props, and even fake corpses outfitted with a variety of wounds and degrees of skin decay. Nonetheless, it's not always easy to unearth a pair of seventeenth-century dueling swords, a nineteenth-century baby carriage, or a boomerang. To find such things quickly and without paying a fortune, you'll have to be resourceful, imaginative, and quick thinking. You'll also need to be very organized. You must be capable of sticking to a tight budget and keeping track of all expenses, including purchases and rentals, shipping and transportation,

Movie studio auctions are a great source for prop buyers and collectors. In the 1960s, MGM (Metro-Goldwyn-Mayer) was the first Hollywood studio to hold a major public auction of its collection of props and costumes *(above)*. Among the items for sale were many treasures from the classic 1939 film *The Wizard of Oz*, including Dorothy's ruby slippers and the Cowardly Lion's costume.

and, of course, cab fares. Also essential is comfortable footwear. (There is so much running around in this job that some prop buyers deduct foot massages as a business-related expense!)

Props are also widely used in television commercials, print advertisements, and photographic layouts for catalogs, magazines, and even packaging (who do you think found those plates and napkins for the photograph on the Lean Cuisine package?). In these cases, many prop buyers, also known as prop stylists, work with or are hired by photographers. When photographers are hired by the art director of a magazine, catalog, or ad agency to shoot a layout or campaign, they usually bring along a prop stylist whom they work with on a regular basis. As a stylist or shopper, you'll need to take orders from the art director and then go hunting for whatever he or she requires for a specific shoot. This often means interpreting what exactly you think the director wants, which can be a challenge. Sometimes your instructions may be vague, such as "Find me a frightening sculpture" or "Get me some delicate Oriental lanterns." Other missions, such as discovering fresh blackberries in December, might seem next to impossible. Relying on your creativity and experience, you'll need to find the object or several options that the director can choose from.

Education and Training

The best way to become a prop buyer is by working—paid or unpaid—as an intern or assistant to learn the ropes on the job. In the world of film, television, and theater, many prop managers or buyers hire assistants to do jobs such as picking

Profile of a Prop Stylist

Originally a fashion merchandiser at a Manhattan department store, Judy Singer has been making a living as an independent prop stylist in New York City for close to three decades. She finds and purchases props that will surround products featured in print advertisements. Her specialty is tabletop styling. Due to Singer's talent for tracking down the perfect pen for any desk or table, she and a photographer with whom she often works are known as the top pen photographer-stylist team in New York.

More often, however, Singer works with food. While the food stylist prepares the food and a carpenter constructs a kitchen set, Singer consults with the art director before going off to purchase dishes, tablecloths, napkins, flowers, and any other objects needed to create the scene the art director wants. Sometimes, interpreting directors' wishes is tricky. She recalls one director who told her he wanted a table out of an Italian movie, with an air of seduction, hand-made pottery, and "really masculine" cheese. Skilled at interpreting what directors want and always up on the latest trends and products, Singer usually shows up with a few potential options. She is present during the photo shoot in case any last-minute prop shopping is required. Having worked for clients ranging from General Electric and Nestlé to *InStyle* and *Bon Appetit* magazines, she says that it's important to put your own taste on hold in order to please your client.

Source: Fireman, Judy. "A Day in the Life of an Independent Professional: A Winning Proposition." 1099 magazine, September 14, 1999. Retrieved July 2005 (http://www.1099.com/c/ar/di/props_d011.html).

up, returning, organizing, and taking care of props. To learn about advertising and print work, assisting stylists, photographers, or art directors is a good introduction to the profession and an excellent way to make contacts. Since getting jobs in this field depends almost exclusively on recommendations and personal references, it is good to make as many contacts as possible. Other related jobs that can be useful include working for a prop or costume rental company.

Salary

The majority of prop buyers are independent workers who are hired on a freelance basis for short-term projects. While you're working, hours are long and intense (fourteen-hour days with

This collection of prop fingers was used in the 1990 horror film *Darkman*. The film's prop master, Kirk Corwin, has worked on major Hollywood productions for over twenty years. Responsible for all aspects of prop use on a film set, he works closely with the script supervisor to make sure props are perfectly placed from one scene to the next.

evening and weekend work are the norm). One week, you might have three assignments where you make $2,000 in three or four days. Then you might spend a month waiting nervously for the phone to ring. Top prop shoppers and stylists with a strong reputation and a list of important clients can earn $800 a day for advertising work and $400 to $500 a day for editorial work in magazines. Prop shoppers who work in film, television, and particularly in theater, earn less, sometimes averaging only between $20,000 and $35,000 a year.

Outlook

Prop shopping is a fairly small field and is quite competitive. Many job opportunities tend to be in large cities where media, art, and publishing industries are located. The secret to success is building up a strong reputation and specializing in a certain type of prop or specific kind of client. Becoming a prop manager, designing and making props, or opening your own prop shop are other related occupations.

FOR MORE INFORMATION

ORGANIZATIONS

International Alliance of Theatrical Stage Employees, Moving Picture Technicians, Artists and Allied Crafts of the United States, Its Territories and Canada (IATSE)
1430 Broadway, 20th Floor
New York, NY 10018
(212) 730-1770
Web site: http://www.iatse-intl.org
> IATSE is the main labor union representing technicians and craftspeople in the entertainment industry, including theater, film, and television.

WEB SITES

Faux Food Diner
http://www.fauxfooddiner.com

This fun Web site is designed to look like a diner. Upon entering, you can order from a menu full of appetizing (fake) foods that make perfect props.

Giant Explorer.com
http://www.giantexplorer.com
Type "Prop shopping" in this Web site's search bar and you will receive lists and reviews of some of the best Web sites available for finding props.

Ketzer.com
http://www.ketzer.com
This site offers original movie props, prop replicas, and film crew items that will interest both buyers and collectors. Includes links to other related archives and sites.

Movie Prop.com
http://www.movieprop.com
Film fans and collectors of movie memorabilia will enjoy this site, which includes props, costumes, and magazines. It also offers information on finding and collecting props for television and movie productions, as well as many useful links and an online store.

Prop People.com Job Board
http://proppeople.com/jobboard.htm
The only online source for job listings that deals exclusively with jobs for "prop people." Includes a discussion board, newsletter, tips, and resources.

Reel Clothes and Props
http://www.reelclothes.com
Reel Clothes sells movie and television costumes and props to the public. The items come from production companies and major studios.

BOOKS

Biederman, Danny. *The Incredible World of Spy-Fi: Wild and Crazy Spy Gadgets, Props, and Artifacts from TV and the Movies.* San Francisco, CA: Chronicle Books, 2004.
The author, a screenwriter who works as an expert consultant to spy-film producers, has collected over 4,000 props from sets of spy movies and television shows. His impressive collection, highlights of which are featured in this book, has been exhibited at the CIA headquarters.

Hemela, Deborah A. *Debbie's Book: The Source Book for Props, Set Dressing and Wardrobe.* 20th ed. Pasadena, CA: Debbies Book, 2005.
Updated yearly, this book provides unique lists of sources and individuals, principally from California but also from around the world, that supply props to the entertainment industry. Props are divided into almost 1,000 categories, ranging from adhesives and African sculptures to special effects and X-rays.

James, Thurston. *The Theater Props What, Where, When: An Illustrated Chronology from Arrowheads to Video Games.* 2nd ed. Studio City, CA: Players Press, 2001.
This title provides everything you need to know about props for the stage.

Reed, Fred. *Show Me the Money! The Standard Catalog of Motion Picture, Television, Stage and Advertising Prop Money.* Jefferson, NC: McFarland & Company, 2005.
Money is often one of the most important props in movies. This original look at how Hollywood makes fake "green stuff" includes interviews with prop masters and displays of over 270 types of movie and stage prop money.

Rogers, Barb. *Costumes, Accessories, Props, and Stage Illusions Made Easy.* Colorado Springs, CO: Meriwether Publishing, 2005.
This book offers inventive approaches to help bring a character to life through imaginative use of props and accessories made from unusual objects.

Sofer, Andrew. *The Stage Life of Props*. Ann Arbor, MI: University of Michigan Press, 2003.
   A fascinating historical exploration that looks at how stage props—from bloody handkerchiefs to pistols—have added meaning to plays.

PERIODICALS

Live Design
249 W. 17th Street
New York, NY 10011
Web site: http://livedesign.com
   Formerly *Entertainment Design*, this magazine offers industry news, features, and interviews with professionals involved in behind-the-scenes theater professions. The Web site includes links to industry resources.

The World of Interiors
Condé Nast U.K.
Vogue House, Hanover Square
London W1S 1JU
England
Web site: http://www.worldofinteriors.co.uk
   Published in England, this influential and informative glossy magazine is considered one of the world's leading sources for stylists, designers, and interior decorators.

2

WARDROBE STYLIST

Why is it that every time you pick up a magazine, log on to the Internet, or turn on the TV, you come face to face with a smashingly dressed celebrity? Famous people have to look good on the red carpet, but did you know that many pay experts to tell them what to wear to the supermarket? In a media culture, where image is everything (and

Wardrobe stylists have to be prepared to work with all kinds of clients—including nonhuman ones. In fact, some stylists actually prefer working with animals. While a few stylists specialize in dressing animals for films and advertisements, others make a living grooming and prettifying dogs, cats, rabbits, monkeys, and even the occasional guinea pig.

best- and worst-dressed lists are everywhere), most high-profile people who spend time in the public eye no longer dare to dress themselves. Instead, they rely on the expert advice and resources of wardrobe stylists.

Job Description

If you love shopping and have an instinctive talent for finding the perfect dress, suit, tie, earrings, handbag, or pair of sunglasses that will make heads turn and flashbulbs go off, being a wardrobe stylist might be the perfect job for you. Most celebrities, particularly Hollywood stars, can't make it through the week without consulting their stylists. However, wardrobe stylists also work to find ideal clothing and accessories for men, women, children, and even animals that are going to appear in films, videos, television programs, commercials, theatrical and musical productions, advertisements, fashion layouts, and magazine spreads. This job can be a creative challenge if you're working on an eighteenth-century French costume drama, a revival of *Grease*, or a science fiction thriller set in the year 3000.

To be a successful stylist, you need a good sense of style and the ability to visualize what kinds of clothing work for a certain person in a specific setting. Attention to detail is important. So is staying up to date with new trends and fashions and knowing what kind of style will appeal to a particular audience.

The majority of stylists work as freelancers. They are hired by photographers; stage, film, or video directors; or art directors for magazines, catalogs, and advertising firms. Your work as a stylist will usually consist of short-term projects. Hours tend to be long, deadlines are tight, and the work atmosphere is creative but stressful. If you have a large wardrobe budget at your disposal, you can have a lot of fun shopping for major designer labels. More often than not, however, small budgets will force you to look for creative solutions. Good business sense and knowing how to manage your time and finances are essential skills.

After hunting down and purchasing the clothes and accessories required, you will be in charge of caring for them and deciding how they will be worn by actors, models, or other clients. As part of an artistic team, you'll have to deal sensitively with the director's ego as well as those of the people wearing the clothes. Stories of clients who refuse to wear a certain suit or gown at the last minute, causing a stylist to seek frantically for an alternate solution, are common. A well-known Hollywood wardrobe stylist once claimed that her favorite actor was a chimpanzee because he didn't talk back to her or drop his clothes all over the floor.

Most stylists get jobs by building up an impressive body of work and a good reputation. A lot of jobs come from word-of-mouth recommendations. It is also important to have a portfolio with samples of your work—either photographs or videos—and a résumé that includes important projects and clients. Many professional stylists have their own agents who book jobs for them and manage their contracts. A fair amount of travel is involved as you will be shuttling from stores and tailors to private homes, studios, theaters, or film sets.

Education and Training

Most stylists have some background in art or fashion. Aside from staying tuned to new trends, it helps to take some courses in art, fashion, or photography at a community college

Stories of a Stylist

Jami had never even heard of a wardrobe stylist until some actress friends told her she'd make a good one. A clothes lover with her own unique style, she volunteered as an apprentice for a well-known stylist, which involved carrying around a lot of heavy shopping bags. Among the insider tips she learned was where to find the best military uniforms and evening wear, which tailors could do overnight alterations, and where she could find clothing for dogs.

In her fourteen-year career, Jami has often come to the rescue in fashion emergencies. One involved an actress who tried to glue in her hair extensions using Krazy Glue. She wound up with her lips glued together and her shirt glued to her chest. Another time—in the days before silicone—Jami had to quickly create a pair of fake breasts out of shoulder pads and duct tape.

Source: Sheppard, Lauren. "Dream Job: Hollywood Wardrobe Stylist." Salary.com. Retrieved July 2005 (http://www.salary.com/careers/ layoutscripts/crel_display.asp?tab=cre&cat=Cat10&ser=Ser71&part=Par157).

For the 2004 action-adventure movie *Troy*, costume director Bob Ringwood studied museum catalogs from all over the world to see what kind of clothes and armor ancient Greeks and Trojans wore in 1200 BC. Then, in four months, he and a team of 150 people designed and created 8,000 costumes and 10,000 pairs of shoes. Above, stars Orlando Bloom and Diane Kruger wear the results of their creative efforts.

or as part of a continuing-education program. You can learn tricks of the trade and make contacts by apprenticing with a professional stylist. Volunteering your services—usually running errands—might eventually lead to a position as a paid assistant. Stylists who work on major film, television, and theater productions often have to be members of the International Alliance of Theatrical Stage Employees, Moving Picture Technicians, Artists and Allied Crafts (IATSE).

Salary

Earnings for stylists vary. Depending on their reputations and client lists, stylists working in the two major markets of New York City and Los Angeles can earn anywhere from $300 to $900 a day. Assistants earn between $150 and $200. This might seem like a lot of money, but many stylists have to deduct health insurance as well as fees paid to agents who get them their jobs. Only top stylists get enough work to keep them constantly busy. Although a few stylists have permanent, full-time jobs, many freelancers go weeks without work. Outside of New York and Los Angeles, fees are lower and work is hard to come by. Aside from consulting with private clients, many stylists also work as makeup artists or hair stylists.

Outlook

The fact that North Americans on the whole are increasingly style-conscious means that people will be willing to spend more money on stylists. In the last fifteen years, stylists have gone from being seen as mere "frock finders" to style gurus who are sought out by celebrities as well as designers who want to promote their clothes and accessories. However, even as stylists become more important, the field is incredibly competitive and remains largely centered in major cities such as New York, Los Angeles, and Toronto.

FOR MORE INFORMATION

ORGANIZATIONS

Association of Stylists and Coordinators
18 E. 18th Street, #5E
New York, NY 10003
Web site: http://www.stylistsasc.com
> This organization's members include some of North America's most talented stylists. The Web site lists their particular specialties and features portfolios with samples of their work.

The International Alliance of Theatrical Stage Employees, Moving Picture Technicians, Artists and Allied Crafts of the United States, Its Territories and Canada (IATSE)
1430 Broadway, 20th Floor
New York, NY 10018
(212) 730-1770
Web site: http://www.iatse-intl.org
> The IATSE is the main labor union representing technicians and craftspeople in the entertainment industry, including theater, film, and television production.

WEB SITES

Photo Talent Online
http://www.phototalentonline.com/index.htm
> Organized by a former stylist who is now an agent for photographers and stylists, this Web site allows you to check out the work of some professionals.

BOOKS

Chierichetti, David. *Edith Head: The Life and Times of Hollywood's Celebrated Costume Designer*. New York, NY: Harper Collins, 2003.

Edith Head spent more than forty years at Paramount, won eight Oscars, and became as famous as the stars—from Grace Kelly to Paul Newman—she dressed. This fascinating biography, which includes many photos of her creations, shows how ambition, talent, and politics contributed to Head's success.

Landis, Deborah Nadoolman. *Costume Design* (Screencraft). Burlington, MA: Focal Press, 2003.
Creating a character through costume is a key aspect of filmmaking. This book features an impressive array of sketches, photos, and interviews with fourteen top international costume designers who have worked on movies ranging from *Shakespeare in Love* to *Batman*.

Sherill, Marcia, and Carey Adina Karmel. *Stylemakers: Inside Fashion*. New York, NY: Monacelli Press, 2002.
An interesting behind-the-scenes look into the world of fashion that includes interviews with more than ninety style makers—from seamstresses, designers and their muses, and trend and color forecasters to publicists, retailers, promoters, and Internet marketers.

PERIODICALS

Elle
Hachette Filipacchi Media
1633 Broadway
New York, NY 10019
Web site: http://www.elle.com
A leading fashion magazine for young women with lively, down-to-earth features on beauty, style, shopping, and runway fashions.

Harper's Bazaar
Hearst Publications
1700 Broadway
New York, NY 10019
Web site: http://www.harpersbazaar.com
A style bible with notes and news on latest trends and fashions, as well as tips for where to shop for them. The fashion editorials are produced by some of the world's leading photographers.

Vogue
Condé Nast Publications
4 Times Square, 17th Floor
New York, NY 10036
Web site: http://www.style.com/vogue
A legendary women's fashion magazine with the world's most elegant and sophisticated clothing and jewelry featured in its glossy pages.

W
Condé Nast Publications
4 Times Square, 17th Floor
New York, NY 10036
Web site: http://www.style.com/w
An oversized fashion and lifestyle magazine with in-depth articles about the international fashion scene accompanied by glamorous photos by the world's top fashion photographers.

ARTICLES

Ginsberg, Merle. "Dressing to Thrill: Wardrobe Stylist Sought by International Fashion Designers." *Los Angeles Magazine*, September 1998. Retrieved July 1998 (http://www.findarticles.com/p/articles/mi_m1346/is_n9_v43/ai_21029536).

3

ANTIQUE DEALER

One of the most popular television programs in North America is PBS's *Antiques Roadshow*. Every week, the show travels to a different city in the United States or Canada. At each stop, people are invited to bring in their family heirlooms, garage sale finds, furnishings, ancient knickknacks, and decorative objects to be evaluated by antique

The popularity of PBS's television program *Antiques Roadshow* reflects North Americans' increasing interest in antiques as collectible objects of beauty and value. Above, appraiser Tara Finley *(left)*, who specializes in antique lead soldiers, dolls, and toys, informs a thrilled Sue Dale of Miami that her penny arcade (a coin-operated machine with games) from the 1920s is worth $700.

specialists. The specialists discover the often fascinating histories of seemingly common or highly unusual objects and the astounding values they sometimes command. This is, in a nutshell, the job of an antique dealer. If you love objects that have a history and think that tracking them down and purchasing them for resale would be an exciting challenge, antique dealing might be an ideal profession.

Job Description

Antique dealers buy and sell antique objects and collector's items. They travel to auctions, flea and antique markets, trade fairs, estate and tag sales, and other dealers' shops, always on the lookout for interesting objects with artistic, historic, and monetary value. After purchasing any antiques, they then sell them to private clients, other dealers, or the public. As a dealer, you can sell your finds from an antique store (yours or another dealer's) or at an antique fair or market. You might even choose to work out of your home, inviting clients to visit you and selling over the Internet.

Dealers often specialize in certain types of antiques. You may decide to focus on toys, silver, furniture, jewelry, books, or film posters. Then again, you may want to deal in objects from a specific era—the late 1800s or the 1920s, for example—or in items that are representative of a certain artistic style, such as baroque or art deco. To become a good dealer, you should begin by deciding what types of antiques really interest you, then learn everything you can about them, including their histories and their potential values. You will need to be able to recognize fraudulent pieces as well as real ones. Aside from having an eye for detail and a honed instinct for finding items, you'll have to spend a lot of time doing careful research. Reading and visiting museums, antique fairs, and other dealers will provide you with some essential background about antiques' histories and their values.

Antiques have no set prices. Their values can change based on factors ranging from condition (perfect or flawed) and rareness (one of a kind or unusual) to importance as historical and artistic objects. Knowledge about such aspects is essential when you negotiate so that you get a good bargain when buying and make a profit when you sell. Good salesmanship and a bit of charm can help you make a larger profit, which in turn will provide you with the capital to invest in more antiques of greater value. In this way, your business will grow and you will attract new customers. In the antique business, building up a large and loyal client base is key to survival. As you gain experience, you can also make money by advising owners on the value of their antiques for insurance or sales purposes. Aside from buying and selling antiques, some dealers work as appraisers for private clients or auction houses.

Traveling around in search of bargains and treasures can be exciting and bring you into contact with many interesting people. However, it can also be expensive and entail a lot of hard work. It is very rare that one stumbles upon a precious object worth tens of thousands of dollars at a garage sale, but the dream of such a find is what inspires many buyers. Traveling, attending events and auctions, and meeting with clients means that antique dealers often work long hours, including evenings and weekends. Depending on the items in which you specialize, you also might have to do a fair amount of lifting and carrying. Used, faded, or damaged objects may need to be cleaned and restored before they can

Steve Hund Jr. owns an antique store in Paxico, Kansas. One of his specialties is vintage stoves. Aside from tracking down, restoring, and selling wood- and coal-burning stoves *(pictured above)* from the end of the nineteenth century, he also sells gas range stoves from the 1930s, 1940s, and 1950s.

be resold. Some antique dealers end up doing some restoration work themselves.

Education and Training

Although a background in art history can be useful, the best way to train for becoming an antique dealer is the do-it-yourself method. This involves reading lots of books, specialized publications, and magazines as well as visiting galleries, museums, and antique stores and markets. Some museums and auction houses offer private training courses.

However, the best education—and the most common way to get started professionally—is to get a job as an apprentice or assistant to an antique dealer. Working in a shop or at an auction house will provide constant exposure to different items as well as to the art of pricing and negotiating. Since the field is fairly competitive, such jobs are not always easy to come by. However, once you get your foot in the door, it is easier to advance in the field. Ultimately, most jobs in the antique world aren't advertised, but they are announced via the professional grapevine. After gaining some experience and clients, many dealers decide to work on their own, gradually building up a collection of objects and a solid client base. You can begin by having a booth at antique fairs or markets or by selling out of your home and eventually open your own business.

Salary

Almost all people who choose to be antique dealers do so out of a love for hunting down and being surrounded by beautiful objects of artistic and historic value. Salaries for those who work for a dealer or auction house are quite low. Working for yourself, your income will depend on a combination of luck, talent, and skill at pricing and negotiating. Most profits you make will need to be invested in more antiques. On the positive side, antiques very rarely lose value. An average starting salary for an antique dealer is around $19,000 a year. After about five years, this increases to $27,000, and after ten to fifteen years, a dealer can make an average of $50,000.

Antique expert Judith Miller examines a ceramic pot that is being sold at Atlantique City, the world's largest antique and collectibles show, which is held twice a year in Atlantic City, New Jersey. An antique collector since the late 1960s, Miller claims there is no secret to appraising antiques. The most important thing is to have a good, critical eye, which can be developed through years of experience and education.

Outlook

Although the antique business is highly competitive and requires a great deal of hard work, negotiation skill, and business savvy (as well as some luck), antiques will always be highly desired items. Unlike financial and art markets, which can fluctuate depending on outside circumstances, new trends, and fashions, antiques are almost always certain to rise in value. A more educated public that increasingly values unique design and fine craftsmanship of the past means that opportunities will continue to grow.

FOR MORE INFORMATION

ORGANIZATIONS

American Society of Appraisers
555 Herndon Parkway, Suite 125
Herndon, VA 20170
(703) 478-2228
Web site: http://www.appraisers.org
> The oldest major organization of professional appraisers. Members are experts in everything from carpets and cars to Asian and African art. The Web site includes links to publications and conferences.

Canadian Antique Dealers' Association
P.O. Box 517, Station K
Toronto, ON M4P 2E0
Canada
(416) 944-9781
Web site: http://www.cadainfo.com
> This association regulates the purchasing of antiques in Canada. Its Web site offers news, links, and a list of shows and events.

Christie's
20 Rockefeller Plaza
New York, NY 10020
(212) 636-2000

http://www.christies.com

In existence since 1766, Christie's is one of the world's major auction houses for antiques and art. The Web site lists auctions and catalogs and offers virtual tours as well as information for buyers, sellers, and those seeking jobs.

The National Antique and Art Dealers Association of America (NAADAA)

220 E. 57th Street
New York, NY 10022
(212) 826-9707
Web site: http://www.naadaa.org

NAADAA is a nonprofit association that represents America's leading art and antique dealers. Its members publish books and articles and organize conferences about art and antiques for dealers and the public.

Sotheby's

1334 York Avenue
New York, NY 10021
(212) 606-7000
Web site: http://search.sothebys.com

This renowned international auction house has been around since 1744. Sotheby's publishes books and catalogs, and provides information about auctions.

WEB SITES

Antique Central

http://www.antique-central.com

An online directory of many antique shops, dealers, auctions, and collectors. You can visit antique stores all over the world, participate in chats and discussion groups, and even send Victorian e-cards to your friends.

Antiques Bulletin On-line
http://www.antiquesbulletin.com
> This site covers many areas of interest within the antiques world, from information about dealers, auctions, and fairs to buying and selling antiques online.

Antique Shop.com
http://www.antique-shop.com
> This online guide to American antique shops, organized according to their specialties, also features an interactive calendar that keeps you up to date on antique-related events.

Antiques Roadshow Online
http://www.pbs.org/wgbh/pages/roadshow
> Antiques Roadshow Online is the companion site to the popular PBS series. This entertaining site features show highlights, appraiser biographies, tips of the trade, appraise-it-yourself games, an interactive *Roadshow* set tour, shopping, and a chance to share your own bargain-hunting stories.

The University of Delaware Library: Early American Antiques
http://www2.lib.udel.edu/usered/elunch/fall2000/antiq/antiq.htm
> A Web source for people interested in early American objects and furniture. Includes lists of antique organizations, events, museums, a reference bookshelf, and an A-to-Z list of antiques.

BOOKS

Brooke, Bob, ed. *How to Start a Home-Based Antiques Business.* 4th ed. Guilford, CT: Globe Pequot, 2005.
> A useful guide on how to set up and run an antique dealership out of your home. It offers advice on locating antiques, pricing, and keeping your business profitable.

Husfloen, Kyle, ed. *Antique Trader Antiques & Collectibles Price Guide 2005.* 20th ed. Iola, WI: Krause Publications, 2004.
> Antique collectors and dealers rely on the yearly update of this exhaustive guide to evaluate treasures ranging from old Raggedy

Ann dolls to vintage pinball machines. It features over 18,000 listings and thousands of color photos to help identify objects.

McKenzie, James W. *Antiques on the Cheap: A Savvy Dealer's Tips: Buying, Restoring, Selling*. North Adams, MA: Storey Publishing, 1998. Practical tips for professional dealers and flea-market addicts on how to find, buy, and sell antiques. The book also includes information on minor repair and restoration work.

PERIODICALS

Antiques Magazine
HP Publishing
2 Hampton Court Road, Harborne
Birmingham B17 9AE
England
Web site: http://www.antiquesmagazine.com
This well-respected weekly magazine is an important guide for serious art collectors, dealers, museums, and others seeking insightful information about fine art and antiques.

Art and Antiques
Trans World Publishing, Inc.
2100 Powers Ferry Road, Suite 300
Atlanta, GA 30339
(770) 955-5656
Web site: http://www.artandantiques.net
A print and online magazine featuring reports, appraisals, events, collectors' forums, and even coverage of thefts in the art and antique world.

Art & Auction
111 8th Avenue, Suite 302
New York, NY 10011
Web site: http://www.artandauction.com/html
This reputed magazine reports on the global art market, covering everything from antiques to contemporary art.

4

ART DEALER

Have you ever strolled through an art gallery and wished that you could buy that beautiful painting, print, or photograph that was hanging on the wall? Sound like a fantasy? Well, if you invest in a career as an art dealer, this dream could become reality. Although for you the fantasy might last only a short while, for your clients the pleasure of owning a unique, valuable, and beautiful work of art could last a lifetime.

Job Description

Art dealers are art lovers who purchase works of art so that other art lovers can then buy and enjoy them. Most art dealers own or work for galleries or have their own private offices where clients visit them. Their clients are generally fairly wealthy individuals interested in acquiring specific works for a private collection or as a financial investment. Sometimes, however, they simply want to decorate homes, offices, or other buildings with original and attractive art. Corporations and institutions such as cultural centers and museums also seek out art dealers, and many large companies collect, invest in, and exhibit art.

Based on your personal interests, as an art dealer you will specialize in certain artists or types of art (watercolor, sculpture, video art, Native American folk art), certain art schools or movements (the impressionists, the New York school), or the art of a certain period or region (eighteenth-century Dutch painting, early twentieth-century American photography). Specializing allows you to focus on a type of art that really interests you and distinguishes you from other dealers who are your competitors. It also narrows down the knowledge required for you to buy wisely and become a reputable dealer.

Being an art dealer is a risky business because the value of art is always changing. In 1990, buyers gathered at Sotheby's auction house in New York to bid on Pierre-Auguste Renoir's 1876 painting entitled *Le Moulin de la Galette*. The work by the renowned French impressionist artist sold for $71 million—the third highest price ever paid for a painting. However, if it were sold again today, appraisers estimate it would be worth only around half as much.

To be constantly aware of what is going on in the art world, especially with respect to the kind of art you buy, you'll frequently be visiting museums, galleries, auctions, and artists' studios as well as reading art journals and publications. You'll also have to be quite sociable, since networking with artists, museum curators, auction houses, and especially collectors and potential clients is an essential part of your job. Ultimately, in the art world, most transactions depend on personal reputation and recommendations. In fact, much of your business—buying and selling—will often be carried out at exhibit openings and other social events. Once you build up a list of clients, you will spend your time seeking out particular works of art that they want for their collections.

Finding art to purchase can be a lot of fun and a great deal of work. It involves reading many books, magazines, and sale catalogs from auction houses, as well as talking with art experts from other galleries and museums. You'll even have to stay alert for news of private collectors who have financial problems or have died; this could lead to the acquisition of an important work of art. Once you find a piece that you or your client is interested in buying, you must be aware of its worth so that you don't pay too much for it. Expert negotiating skills are crucial.

Education and Training

There are numerous ways to become an art dealer. Many dealers take courses or have college degrees in art history, but the surest route is probably on-the-job experience. In this competitive business, most people start out at the bottom, doing basic work—answering phones, doing research, and carefully packing and storing art—as volunteers. Getting a job as an intern or an assistant at a gallery, museum, or auction house is a great way to start. You will learn about art

Different Dealers

There are various types of art dealers:

Primary-market dealers discover fresh talent and help advance the careers of unknown artists by showing their works at galleries. This job includes meeting many new people and visiting artists at work in their studios.

Art dealers travel a good deal, attending events, auctions, and trade fairs in search of interesting works for their clients. Held every spring in Manhattan, Artexpo New York is considered the largest art fair in the world and features paintings, photography, sculptures, and other works by over 2,000 artists. With close to 50,000 art professionals in attendance, it also provides an important opportunity to network and make new contacts.

Second-market dealers handle works that have come on the market because of resale. If one of these dealers knows that a client—a private collector, museum, or other institution—is interested in such a work and it is within the dealer's area of expertise, he or she can negotiate its purchase.

Private dealers work in their own offices and meet with clients on an appointment-only basis. Private dealers can give more personalized attention to clients, educating them about works; visiting artists' studios, galleries, and art fairs with them; doing appraisals; and even attending auctions on their behalf.

Art consultants help inexperienced collectors make purchasing decisions by offering expert advice, taking them around to galleries, and helping them negotiate. Unlike dealers, consultants don't keep an inventory of artists' works. They earn a commission (paid by the buyer, seller, or even both parties) when they succeed in closing a deal.

and the business of buying and selling, and you will make contacts with artists and clients. Before opening their own galleries, many dealers work as curators in museums or auction houses, or as assistants at other people's galleries.

Dealers often visit artists at work in their workshops and studios. Above, an artist at Joseph Bronze Works in Joseph, Oregon, is creating a bronze statue of a bear. A former lumber town, Joseph currently has several foundries that specialize in bronze statue casting, in which bronze is poured into a mold and left to solidify into a sculpted form.

Salary

As a dealer, much of your revenue will go toward maintaining your gallery. What is left over is your "salary." The amount can vary enormously depending on the state of the art market, the health of the economy, and your ability to attract good artists and loyal clients. If you represent new artists, you'll often exhibit their work on consignment. When a work is purchased, they will receive money while you receive a commission based on the sale. In other cases, you might be hired by a client to purchase a certain piece that isn't in your gallery, in which case you will receive a commission that might be between 7 and 10 percent of the work's price. In general, dealers who are starting out make around $25,000 a year. If you survive starting up and develop a good reputation, you can eventually earn $100,000 or even much more.

Outlook

Art will always be a hot commodity, but the art market can be very unstable due to changing tastes, trends, and the economy. Even successful dealers can see their fortunes rise and fall over time. In 1990, for example, the art market crashed. Prices fell by 30 to 50 percent. In New York City, a major art center, 70 of the city's 500 galleries went out of business. Nevertheless, established dealers with solid reputations can enjoy long, successful careers.

FOR MORE INFORMATION

ORGANIZATIONS
Art Dealers Association of America (ADAA)
575 Madison Avenue
New York, NY 10022

(212) 940-8590
Web site: http://www.artdealers.org
This nonprofit organization of leading art dealers is a good source for information about artists, galleries, catalogs and publications (print and online), collectors' resources, and appraisal services.

Art Dealers Association of Canada (ADAC)
111 Peter Street, Suite 501
Toronto, ON M5V 2H1
Canada
(416) 934-1583
Web site: http://www.ad-ac.ca
The largest association of art galleries in Canada, whose members represent the country's leading artists. The ADAC offers information about Canadian and international artists and dealers, markets, events, publications, and employment opportunities.

The National Antique and Art Dealers Association of America (NAADAA)
220 E. 57th Street
New York, NY 10022
(212) 826-9707
Web site: http://www.naadaa.org
NAADAA is a nonprofit association that represents America's leading art and antique dealers. Its members publish books and articles and organize conferences about art and antiques for dealers and the public.

WEB SITES

Art Dealers Association of America's Collector's Guide to Working with Art Dealers
http://www.artdealers.org/collectors/guide/adaa.guide.pdf
ADAA's online guide offers easy-to-understand information about

the art world and the role of art dealers. It includes tips for buying and selling art to a dealer, as well as at auctions and online.

Art Info
http://www.artinfo.com
The most comprehensive source of art news on the Web—for anyone curious about art. Information includes a worldwide calendar of events and exhibits; links to books, magazines, and artists' sites; and games, puzzles, and quizzes for kids and adults.

BOOKS

De Coppet, Laura. *The Art Dealers, Revised and Expanded: The Powers Behind the Scene Tell How the Art World Really Works*. Lanham, MD: Cooper Square Press, 2002.
In personal anecdotes and essays, fifty-five prominent art dealers talk about the difficult and fascinating aspects of their trade.

Goldstein, Malcolm. *Landscape with Figures: A History of Art Dealing in the United States*. New York, NY: Oxford University Press, 2000.
This history of art dealing in the United States, from eighteenth-century portrait salesmen in the thirteen colonies to the high-rolling gallery owners of today, helps explain why America currently boasts the world's biggest art market.

Neuberger, Roy R. *The Passionate Collector: Eighty Years in the World of Art*. Hoboken, NJ: John Wiley & Sons, 2002.
A renowned art collector, Neuberger has shared much of his private collection with important American museums. In this vivid portrait of the twentieth-century American art scene, he mixes personal memories with art history.

PERIODICALS

Art & Auction
111 8th Avenue, Suite 302
New York, NY 10011

Web site: http://www.artandauction.com/html
   This reputed magazine reports on the global art market, covering everything from antiques to contemporary art. It includes information on artists and exhibitions, analysis of market trends, reviews, previews, and listings of auctions and antique shows.

Art in America
575 Broadway
New York, NY 10012
(212) 941-2800
Web site: http://www.artinamericamagazine.com
   A monthly print magazine that explores the art scene in America and abroad. Articles and reviews on everything from classical painting and avant-garde photography to important new books, as well as profiles of fresh talent.

Canadian Art
51 Front Street East, Suite 210
Toronto, ON M5E 1B3
Canada
Web site: http://www.canadianart.ca
   A quarterly print magazine with insightful articles on Canadian and international visual art accompanied by high-quality reproductions. Also features a critical guide to art exhibitions and events throughout Canada.

Gallery Guide
97 Grayrock Road
P.O. Box 5541
Clinton, NJ 08809-5541
Web site: http://www.galleryguide.com
   A comprehensive and current source of gallery and museum exhibitions in the United States, with news, artists profiles, openings, highlights, and even maps to guide you to galleries off the beaten track.

5

RETAIL BUYER

Have you ever wondered what it would be like to shop on a large scale (spending hundreds of thousands of dollars) and get paid for it? Not for yourself, of course, but for the owners of a retail store. Imagine purchasing hundreds of toys, thousands of chocolate bars, or a few dozen designer dresses that you glimpsed upon the fashion runways

Clothing buyers for major department stores rarely miss the seasonal fashion shows in which leading designers reveal their latest creations. Although the clothes paraded down the runway are incredibly expensive, they often provide valuable clues to upcoming trends. Above, Canadian model Linda Evangelista shows off an outfit designed by the legendary French fashion house Christian Dior.

of New York, Paris, and Milan. If you find the notion appealing, consider that such buying sprees are a major part of the job of a retail buyer.

Job Description

Retail buyers are in charge of selecting and purchasing merchandise for individual stores and boutiques, for companies that run chain stores such as CVS and Macy's, and for discount stores like Target and Wal-Mart. Some buyers also purchase goods and products that are sold through catalogs or over the Internet. In general, buyers specialize in a specific type of product, such as men's shoes, children's books, or silverware. Often, the larger the store, the more specialized the buyers.

As a large-scale retail buyer, you won't usually go out shopping for products. In most cases, you'll work at the main business office of your company or store. Buyers for small stores often work in the store itself. If you're purchasing manufactured goods such as clothing, furniture, appliances, toys, cosmetics, or packaged goods, you'll often order them directly from the manufacturer. Other products, such as clothing, accessories, fresh fish, meat, fruit, vegetables, plants, and flowers, you'll probably buy from wholesalers. Wholesalers buy goods from many different individual suppliers, such as farms or craftspeople, and resell them to retail buyers in very large quantities.

Retail buyers don't simply decide what to buy based on their own tastes. Careful research must be done about what the buying public, and specifically the public that shops in your store, wants. Aside from knowing who your customers are and what kind of tastes and budgets they have, you also have to be aware of market trends, new products, and the state of the economy in general—factors that can change

Success Is Sweet

Retail buyers don't always start out with a specialization. However, depending on their interests and the needs of their employers, they often end up focusing on a par-

ticular area. Take Valeria Stansfield, for example. She specializes in candy. In fact, she buys candy and snacks for the Rite Aid chain of drug stores in the United States. Stansfield's purchasing decisions have an impact on the candy that is sold in more than

Buyers don't simply purchase merchandise—they also often come up with strategies on how to sell it. The idea to sell gumballs out of a gigantic machine in the middle of a shopping mall is a sure (and original) way to attract young clients.

3,600 stores in over thirty states. Ironically, when Stansfield was a student, she had hopes of becoming a dentist. Instead, she began her retail career as a buyer of children's clothing and then switched, in 1978, to another popular children's item—and a dentist's worst enemy—candy.

Stansfield credits her success as a buyer to several factors. She is always willing to try new products, providing the manufacturers can prove why their goods are so great. She also stays attuned to the diverse tastes and buying patterns in various markets. For example, she has discovered that people on the East Coast do not have the same preferences as those on the West Coast. Consequently, she buys different product mixes for stores in different regions. Last but not least, Stansfield loves candy! There isn't any candy sold in any of the 3,600 drug stores that she hasn't sucked, crunched, or bitten into.

Source: "Workin' Hard, Lovin' Candy." Professional Candy Buyer, May–June 2001. Retrieved July 2005 (http://www. retailmerchandising.net/candy/archives/0601/0601rit.asp).

daily. A lot can be learned from visiting trade fairs and suppliers, reading trade journals, and also checking out the competition. Buyers spend considerable time shopping around for products to see which manufacturers or wholesalers offer the best prices, quality, and variety. Some buyers, especially fashion buyers who must stay up on the latest runway trends, even travel abroad.

Forging close relationships with suppliers is another important part of a buyer's job. You'll need to negotiate good prices with suppliers and make sure they can deliver on time. Deciding what items shoppers will want, how many to buy, and at what price they should be sold can be exciting but stressful. If your estimates are wrong, the store will be left with a surplus of unsold merchandise. The store will lose money and you'll be largely to blame. If, however, customers buy the items you choose, the store, or at least your department, will make profits.

Education and Training

Increasingly, due to a competitive market, retail buyers require a BA in business or marketing, or some related courses at a community college. However, many stores and companies, particularly smaller ones, favor employees who have worked their way up through various retail positions. In fact, many buyers start out working in stores where they gain retail experience and are then hired as assistant or junior

Some large chain stores, such as Toys "R" Us, employ two types of buyers. Planners are in charge of the numbers side of buying—deciding how much to order, which stores to send items to, and when to send them. Creative merchandisers, often called "buyers," decide what products go into stores, how to price them, and how and where to display them on shelves and in aisles.

buyers. A lot of major chain stores, such as JCPenney and Wal-Mart, have their own in-house buyer training programs for employees. After training as an assistant or junior buyer, you can be promoted to an associate buyer, in charge of purchases for a specific section of a store. Over time, you can then become a full-fledged buyer who, aside from purchasing for an entire department, supervises associate buyers and interns. At the top of the purchasing pyramid are senior buyers and purchasing directors, whose function is to oversee all retail purchases for a store or company.

Salary

Assistant or junior buyers who are starting out can earn about $20,000 to $25,000 a year. Depending on the store and the length of time they've been working, associate buyers and full-fledged buyers might earn anywhere between $30,000 and $60,000 a year. Senior buyers for large retailers or department stores can earn $70,000 a year or more. Although earnings can be high, an average work week can often surpass forty hours, particularly around the holidays, when working late nights and weekends is common. Of course, an added bonus is that you usually receive some good discounts on store merchandise!

Outlook

Retail jobs in general are dependent on the state of the economy. When the economy is booming, consumers spend more and stores therefore need more buyers to purchase merchandise. In a poor economy, retailers tend to cut back on employees. With regard to the long-term future, opportunities for retail buyers will probably become scarcer. As big chains expand and replace smaller, independent stores, fewer buyers are responsible for a larger number of stores. Meanwhile, computers and technology are able to perform and simplify many tasks—such as accounting, ordering, tracking shipments, and maintaining inventory—that were formerly done by buyers. As a result, a single buyer can do the work previously done by two or three people.

FOR MORE INFORMATION

ORGANIZATIONS

National Retail Federation (NRF)
325 7th Street NW, Suite 1100
Washington, DC 20004
(800) NRF-HOW2 (673-4692) or (202) 783-7971
Web site: http://www.nrf.com
> The world's largest retail trade association represents an industry with more than 1.4 million retail establishments and more than 23 million employees in the United States.

Retail Council of Canada (RCC)
1255 Bay Street, Suite 800
Toronto, ON M5R 2A9
Canada
(416) 922-6678
Web site: http://www.retailcouncil.org
> The voice of Canadian retail, RCC represents department stores, mass merchants, specialty chains, and independent and online stores throughout Canada. Its Web site lists industry news and information about events, education, and resources.

WEB SITES

Apparel News.Net
http://www.apparelnews.net

> Everything a buyer needs to know about the fashion industry appears here, including news, information on fashion and trade shows, trends, and useful industry links.

Canadian Retail Institute
http://www.retaileducation.ca

> Whether you're a retail employer, educator, student, or someone seeking a career in retail, this institute funded by the Canadian government is a great resource.

Retail Merchandising
http://www.retailmerchandising.net

> A Web site with links and information for people who work in the retail industry. Includes links on starting and running a business, sales and marketing, and useful services and organizations.

BOOKS

Bohlinger, Maryanne Smith. *Merchandise Buying*. 5th ed. New York, NY: Fairchild Books, 2001.
> A textbook that introduces basic buying and merchandising principles, each illustrated with real-life case studies.

Clodfelter, Richard. *Retail Buying: From Basics to Fashion*. 2nd ed. New York, NY: Fairchild Books, 2002.
> Step-by-step instructions for retail buyers on tasks such as identifying and understanding potential customers, forecasting sales, negotiating, monitoring inventory, pricing, and promotion.

Corstjens, Judith, and Marcel Corstjens. *Store Wars: The Battle for Mindspace and Shelfspace*. Hoboken, NJ: John Wiley & Sons, 1999.
> An interesting analysis of various issues in contemporary retailing, with specific focus upon the grocery trade and conflicts between manufacturers and retailers.

Goworek, Helen. *Fashion Buying*. Malden, MA: Blackwell Science, 2002.
    This book covers the profession of buying clothing, footwear, and
    accessories.
Underhill, Paco. *Call of the Mall*. New York, NY: Simon & Schuster, 2004.
    An intelligent, humorous, and in-depth study of America's gift to
    consumers: the mall. Mall rat Underhill takes readers on a tour to
    see how and why retailers do what they do and how consumers
    respond.
Varley, Rosemary. *Retail Product Management: Buying and
    Merchandising*. New York, NY: Routledge, 2001.
    A clear, basic textbook for anyone studying retail product manage-
    ment or buying and merchandising.

PERIODICALS

Canadian Retailer
Retail Council of Canada
1255 Bay Street, Suite 800
Toronto, ON M5R 2A9
Canada
Web site: http://www.retailcouncil.org/cdnretailer
    This bimonthly magazine published by the Retail Council of
    Canada provides up-to-date industry research, analysis, and advice
    about diverse retail topics.

STORES
325 7th Street NW, Suite 1100
Washington, DC 20004
Web site: http://www.stores.org
    This retail industry magazine provides news, buying guides, and
    information on top global and domestic retailers and specialty stores.

6

PURCHASING AGENT

Like retail buyers, purchasing agents get paid to go shopping on a grand scale. The main difference is that while retail buyers shop for products that will then be bought by the public, purchasing agents buy supplies for companies and manufacturers. If you like the wheeling and dealing of buying but not the stress of having to deal directly with changing consumer and marketing trends, you might want to consider a career as a purchasing agent.

Job Description

Manufacturers, businesses, and even governments rely on purchasing agents to track down everything they need to make goods or provide services. Factories, for example, depend upon purchasers to find quality materials at bargain prices so they can produce goods that are essential to the nation's economy. Many purchasing agents work in a specific industry, such as construction, electronics, communications, clothing, automobile, or metal or chemical fabrication. Based on production schedules, they have to make sure that the right quantity of raw materials or supplies is being delivered to a manufacturer in order to keep production lines constantly moving. If you work in the clothing industry, for example, you'll be buying fabric, buttons, zippers, and other materials that are used to make clothes. If you work in the automobile industry, you'll be purchasing parts and materials—ranging from steel, tires, and spark plugs to engines and windows—used to assemble cars. Obviously, before you actually make a purchase, you'll have to know a considerable amount about the relevant supplies or materials.

Being a purchasing agent is a dynamic but high-pressure profession. If materials arrive damaged or late, or if you order too much or too little of an item, your company can lose

Thousands of products are made from recyclable and durable plastic vinyl—from water pipes and telephone cords to credit cards and plastic bags. Above, a purchasing agent visits a factory that manufactures vinyl film and sheet products of various thicknesses whose uses range from textured wall coverings to flexible food wrap.

money and credibility. If, however, you succeed in buying top-quality materials at rock-bottom prices and they arrive on time, you and your company can make a good profit.

Like retail buyers, purchasing agents must do an enormous amount of research before deciding what supplies to buy, in what quantity, and from whom. Talking with coworkers and studying your company's sales records, sales projections, and inventory levels will help you decide how much and what you need to buy. Reading industry publications and meeting with suppliers will help you decide with whom to do business. Getting together with suppliers often entails some traveling, occasionally even outside of the country. Being both an effective communicator and an excellent negotiator are key to cutting deals and signing purchasing contracts that will benefit your company.

Some purchasing agents work for city, state, provincial, and federal governments. They are responsible for buying supplies and choosing service providers that

The world's finest perfume makers purchase the fragrant oil that is distilled from rose petals. The largest supply of commercially grown roses comes from Bulgaria, where workers cultivate the musk rose, a light red flower that has thirty-six petals and a very strong fragrance. It takes 60,000 of these roses to make a single ounce of rose oil.

are essential to the running of various government departments and agencies. For instance, you might need to contract a company to deliver office supplies, do construction work, or provide cleaning services for a government office building. You'll do this by reviewing bids and offers, often over the Internet, from various suppliers. Government purchasing agents have to follow strict rules when awarding contracts to avoid charges of favoritism.

Successful purchasing agents can be promoted to purchasing managers. Managers are in charge of supervising more complex buying operations as well as monitoring and training all agents and assistant or junior buyers. As a manager, you are ultimately responsible for all purchase decisions and the positive or negative effects they have on the company's fortunes.

Education and Training

Increasingly, many employers look for purchasing agents who have a college degree in business or economics. However, technical training or background in the industry in which you plan to work can also give you an edge. For example, knowing about computers and their parts can be a definite advantage if you want to become a purchasing agent for a computer manufacturer. Getting a part-time job or working as an intern to a purchaser can provide training and experience. Many companies have in-house training programs for purchasing agents where you can learn all about pricing, markets, and suppliers.

Since the job market for purchasing agents and managers is competitive, it can help if you are professionally certified. The American Purchasing Society, the Institute for Supply Management, and the Purchasing Management

Buyers who think creatively can save their employers money while coming up with environmentally friendly solutions. Purchasing agents for several U.S. specialty paper manufacturers discovered an alternative to making paper from wood pulp: using leftover blue jeans. As a result, instead of throwing away a million pounds of scrap denim every year, Levi's jeans factory workers in New Mexico save the scraps so they can be sold to companies that recycle them into paper products.

Association of Canada all offer certification based on education, work experience, and a written exam. Many U.S. government agencies require certification through the National Institute of Governmental Purchasing.

Salary

While many purchasing agents work more than forty hours a week, they are quite well compensated for their efforts.

On average, purchasing agents earn around $45,000 a year. Salaries for those starting out hover around $20,000, but those with more experience can eventually earn over $70,000. Purchasing managers earn an average yearly salary of $50,000, and with time, they can expect to earn over $80,000.

Outlook

Jobs for purchasing agents and managers are not expected to increase in the future. Aside from a greater tendency to centralize buying decisions at a company's main headquarters, the primary reason for this lack of growth is the increasing efficiency of technology. Computer software can track inventory, measure sales and stock levels, and automatically reorder supplies from manufacturers. Meanwhile, the Internet has simplified communication and research and allows contract bidding and purchases to be carried out electronically.

FOR MORE INFORMATION

ORGANIZATIONS

American Purchasing Society
P.O. Box 256
Aurora, IL 60506
(630) 859-0250

Web site: http://www.american-purchasing.com
A national association of buyers and purchasing managers that offers training, online courses, and recognized certification programs for becoming a certified purchasing professional (CPP) and a certified professional purchasing manager (CPPM). The Web site has information about seminars, books, and finding jobs.

Federal Acquisition Institute (FAI)
U.S. General Services Administration
c/o Defense Acquisition University
9820 Belvoir Road
Fort Belvoir, VA 22060-5565
(703) 805-2300
Web site: http://www.fai.gov
FAI provides online courses, training, resources, and other tools to promote purchasing skills and knowledge. It also publishes information on purchasing trends and policies.

Institute for Supply Management (ISM)
P.O. Box 22160
Tempe, AZ 85285-2160
(800) 888-6276 or (480) 752-6276
Web site: http://www.ism.ws
ISM provides education with respect to the purchasing and supply management profession.

National Institute of Governmental Purchasing (NIGP)
151 Spring Street
Herndon, VA 20170-5223
(800) FOR-NIGP (367-6447) or (703) 736-8900
Web site: http://www.nigp.org
This nonprofit organization offers support to those working in the public sector purchasing profession. NIGP provides services including

education, professional networking, research, and technical assistance for purchasing agents throughout the United States and Canada.

Purchasing Management Association of Canada
2 Carlton Street, Suite 1414
Toronto, ON M5B 1J3
Canada
(416) 977-7111
Web site: http://www.pmac.ca
Canada's leading association for purchasing agents offers training, education, and professional development, including professional purchaser certification.

BOOKS

Ashley, James M. *International Purchasing Handbook*. New York, NY: Simon & Schuster, 1998.
Sometimes the best way to obtain cost reductions is to purchase supplies from international sources. This book provides all the information needed to make purchases from outside North America while sidestepping potential problems.

Cavinato, Joseph L., and Ralph G. Kauffman. *The Purchasing Handbook: A Guide for the Purchasing and Supply Professional*. 6th ed. New York, NY: McGraw-Hill, 1999.
For the last thirty years, this book has been an important reference for purchasing professionals throughout the world. A wide range of topics are explored by more than 100 top purchasing authorities.

Hough, Harry E., and James M. Ashley. *Purchasing Fundamentals for Today's Buyer*. Englewood Cliffs, NJ: Prentice Hall, 1992.
Although a little outdated, many purchasers still swear by this informative book full of ideas on how to make buying easier and more profitable. It is particularly useful for purchasing assistants and junior buyers who are just starting out.

Neef, Dale. *E-Procurement: From Strategy to Implementation.*
Englewood Cliffs, NJ: Prentice Hall, 2001.
This book examines how Internet buying is revolutionizing
business-to-business purchasing and offers advice and strategies
for professionals.

Nelson, Dave, Patricia E. Moody, and Jonathan Stegner. *The
Purchasing Machine: How the Top Ten Companies Use Best Practices
to Manage Their Supply Chains.* New York, NY: Free Press, 2001.
The authors, all professionals in the purchasing field, investigate
the various purchasing strategies used by top companies, examin-
ing their successes and flaws.

PERIODICALS

Purchasing
225 Wyman Street
Waltham, MA 02451
Web site: http://www.purchasing.com
This bimonthly print and online trade magazine offers timely and
in-depth reports for purchasing professionals in the United States
and Canada.

Purchasing b2b
Rogers Media
One Mount Pleasant Road, 7th Floor
Toronto, ON M4Y 2Y5
Canada
Web site: http://www.bizlink.com/purchasingB2B.htm
Purchasing b2b is a print and online magazine offering news,
expert analysis, and profiles of Canadian purchasing professionals.

7

PERSONAL SHOPPER

Do you have friends or relatives who open their closets and announce that they have nothing to wear, or who spend hours agonizing over how to dress for a party or a job interview? When they go to a department store, do they get stressed by crowds and frustrated by the fact that they can't tell what looks good in those tiny fitting rooms? Do you know people who dread birthdays and holi-days because it means spending hours searching for gifts that they know will just end up being exchanged? All of these problems are so common that they have led to the cre-ation of a new profession: personal shopping. If you have a knack for shopping and have never experienced any of the frustrations and dilemmas listed here, you might make a great personal shopper.

Job Description

Personal shoppers shop for people who don't have the time, the patience, or the skills to shop for themselves. Many personal shoppers specialize in shopping for clothing and accessories. Their clients are usually people with high-profile jobs—artists, media figures, business people, and politi-cians—who are seen and judged by the public. Based on their body types, personalities, jobs, and lifestyles, you'll first help your clients discover what kind of styles and colors suit them. This involves knowing a good deal about fashion as well as different professions and social occasions (the proper attire for a lawyer is different from that of a rock star, best-selling author, or ambassador). You'll also need to understand people and their needs, insecurities, and sensitiv-ities. Patience and tact are essential for a personal shopper.

Most personal shoppers are freelancers who work with clients on an individual basis. Some jobs might be one-time

projects. For instance, a television journalist wants to change her image and update her wardrobe. You might begin with a consultation at her home where you both go through her closet and decide which clothes look good on her and which don't. Some articles can be given away, while others might be altered. Then, based on your client's measurements, needs, and budget, you'll go on a shopping spree. It helps to have good personal relationships with designers and retailers at department stores and boutiques. Often, you can work out an agreement whereby you can return or exchange clothes that don't fit or suit your client. Sometimes, you can even get discounts.

After bringing back your finds to your client, you will both "edit" the new wardrobe, deciding what to keep, what to return, and what needs tailoring. Some shoppers help accessorize clothing with jewelry, shoes, and bags, and work with clients on how to create different looks by mixing pieces. Making someone look and feel good about him- or herself can be very gratifying. If pleased with your work, some people

Personal shoppers and stylists to Hollywood stars are very powerful people, especially around Oscar time. With celebrities counting on shoppers' style savvy and fashion designers competing for A-list actresses to model their clothes on the red carpet, the pressure is on. Often months before the awards, stylists visit designers and reserve particular one-of-a-kind gowns for their clients, thus keeping them out of the hands of competing celebrity shoppers.

Increasingly, people who don't have time to go grocery shopping are relying on the Internet for their groceries. One of the most successful online grocers is Peapod.com. After customers choose from 11,000 items (including prepared foods, wine, and beer) from the Peapod Web site, personal shoppers are sent to handpick groceries at local markets and deliver them right to a client's door.

might become permanent clients. They'll call you if they need a special outfit for an awards ceremony, some suits for a business trip, or even back-to-school clothes for their kids. Some people even seek out shoppers for advice on what to wear at a criminal court trial or when getting a divorce.

Some personal shoppers shop for items other than clothes. For many people, purchasing presents—particularly around the holidays when stores are packed and shopping lists seem endless—can be stressful and time consuming. Many corporations also rely on personal shoppers when they need to buy gifts for clients, suppliers, and employees.

Although most personal shoppers have their own businesses, some work for shopping malls or large department stores such as Macy's, Bergdorf Goodman, and Neiman Marcus, all of whom offer personal shopping services. Customers who want wardrobe advice and individual attention—and often access to private fitting rooms—rely on these personal shoppers. Personal shoppers often receive a commission or a shopper's fee along with their salary.

Education and Training

To be a good personal shopper, you need to know everything there is to know about fashion and new products. Reading books and staying up to date with trends via magazines and style reports is essential. So is going to shops and talking to retailers. You'll need to be aware of what is available (and for how much) from sources as diverse as major department stores, vintage boutiques, sample sales, new designer fairs, and Web sites. Some professional shoppers offer seminars and courses for people who want to get into the field.

The best way to gain knowledge and work experience is to get a job in retail sales. Even working weekends in a local boutique gives you insight into customers' personalities and

Tale of Two Shoppers

Mary Walbridge is a costume designer for film and television in Los Angeles. She has been nominated for two Emmy Awards as a costume supervisor for the television show *Will & Grace*. Walbridge is also a stylist and personal shopper who has shopped for celebrities such as Matt Damon, Michael Douglas, and Demi Moore. Walbridge offers general shopping services for bridal and holiday parties, black-tie events, and career changes. Per hour, she charges $250 for a consultation and $100 for shopping. Shoppers with experience and clients such as Walbridge's can make around $100,000 a year.

Laurie Ely of Chicago stumbled onto personal shopping by accident. When she bought groceries at the supermarket, Ely was often approached by elderly people who couldn't read labels or reach items. Divorced and with three children to feed, Ely made flyers announcing the services of "Laurie the Shopping Lady," which she posted around her neighborhood. Before long, she had such a long client list that grocery shopping came to mean pushing five carts. By charging 15 percent commission plus an $8 shopping fee, she earns about $20,000 a year.

Source: www.yourownpersonalshopper.com and www.entreprenuer.com/article/0,4621,319274,00.html.

shopping patterns and allows you to hone your advising skills. In the meantime, there is no reason you can't offer your shopping services to friends and family members.

Salary

Salaries for professional shoppers vary enormously based on the amount and type of projects available and clients' budgets. A shopper could earn anywhere from $20,000 to $50,000 a year. Very resourceful full-time personal shoppers with their own businesses and a few celebrity clients can make more.

Outlook

To date, the professional shopping field is quite small. This means that while there is a lot of competition, there is also opportunity for enterprising shoppers. People who need individual attention in a society where time is increasingly precious will continue to benefit from the services of personal shoppers.

FOR MORE INFORMATION

ORGANIZATIONS
Association of Image Consultants International
431 East Locust Street, Suite 300
Des Moines, IA 50309

(515) 282-5500
Web site: http://www.aici.org
> With local chapters throughout the United States and Canada, this organization promotes image consulting as a profession and provides education, training, job resources, and reports on new trends and fashions to those who work in the field, including personal shoppers.

WEB SITES

CEO Express Marketplace
http://www.ceoexpress.com/html/pmarketplace.asp
> This Web page is a great resource for personal shoppers, with online shopping links to all sorts of items organized by category and occasion.

Your Personal Shopper
http://www.your-shopper.com/home.html
> A network of personal shoppers who satisfy shopping needs for both individuals and businesses on a wide variety of occasions.

BOOKS

Andre, Mary Lou. *Ready to Wear: An Expert's Guide to Choosing and Using Your Wardrobe.* New York, NY: Perigee Books, 2004.
> Fashion consultant and wardrobe manager Andre provides answers to the question "What to wear?"

Halbreich, Betty. *Secrets of a Fashion Therapist: What You Can Learn Behind the Dressing Room Door.* New York, NY: HarperCollins, 2000.
> Halbreich has spent over twenty years giving fashion advice to female shoppers at New York's elegant Bergdorf Goodman department store. In this often humorous book, she shares anecdotes and offers tips on how to deal with everything from casual Fridays to black-tie affairs.

Lumpkin, Emily S. *Get Paid to Shop: Be a Personal Shopper for Corporate America.* Columbia, SC: Forte Publishing, 1999.
> Advice on how to start your own home-based personal shopping business.

McBride, Laura Harrison. *FabJob Guide to Become a Personal Shopper*. Seattle, WA: FabJob.com, 2003.
> A guide on how to make a living as a personal shopper. Industry experts offer advice on how to get hired and tips on getting discounts and opening your own personal shopping business.

Sparklesoup Studios. *Career KNOWtes: Personal Shopping* (How to Have Fun and Make Money in a Career You Love). Irving, TX: Sparklesoup Studios, 2004.
> A practical guide on how to get started as a personal shopper and where to find jobs.

Taggart, Judy, and Jackie Walker. *I Don't Have a Thing to Wear: The Psychology of Your Closet*. New York, NY: Simon & Schuster, 2003.
> A fun and useful book by two fashion experts that offers tips, hints, and quizzes related to how women can come to terms with and transform their wardrobes.

PERIODICALS

Domino

Condé Nast Publications
4 Times Square, 17th Floor
New York, NY 10036
Web site: http://www.dominomag.com
> This print magazine describes itself as a personal shopper. Specializing in items for the home in a variety of styles and price ranges, it also features exclusive giveaways and discounts.

Lucky

Condé Nast Publications
4 Times Square, 17th Floor
New York, NY 10036
Web site: http:www.luckymag.com
> A shopping magazine that helps you track down anything you might desire, from clothing and cosmetics to housewares and furnishings—anywhere in the world. Each issue features a different

city and its most interesting shops. A handy toll-free number allows you to call for help if you're having trouble finding items listed in the magazine.

ARTICLES

Barker, Olivia. "School Shopping Goes Pro." *USA Today*, August 22, 2004. Retrieved July 2005 (http://www.usatoday.com/life/lifestyle/2004-08-22-school-shopping_x.htm).

Critchell, Samantha. "Personal Shopper Says Your Attitude Trumps Your Outfit." *Detroit Free Press*, June 23, 2005. Retrieved July 2005 (http://www.freep.com/features/living/dressingroom23w_20050623.htm).

Henricks, Mark. "Starting a Business as a Personal Shopper." Entrepreneur.com, December 23, 2004. Retrieved July 2005 (http://www. entrepreneur.com/article/0,4621,319274,00.html).

MYSTERY SHOPPER

Have you ever imagined what it would be like if you could spend your days buying clothes, seeing movies, working out at health clubs, and eating in popular restaurants? Does the thought seem appealing? Now imagine getting paid to do all these things. It might sound like a fantasy or a put-on, but thousands of people across North

In the United States, client firms hire close to 800 mystery shopping companies to recruit mystery shoppers. Although the field is growing, mystery shopping is a competitive business. To gain an edge, some shoppers take training and certification courses. By understanding how the industry works and being very observant while they are shopping, mystery shoppers can make sure they are the first ones companies call with new assignments.

America are supplementing their incomes and even making a living by going shopping. Because they do so undercover, they are known as mystery shoppers.

Job Description

You've probably heard the saying "The customer is king." Unfortunately, not all businesses can be sure that their clients

Alter Egos

Mystery shoppers are also known as:
    Auditors
    Consumer researchers
    Customer service researchers
    Market researchers
    Scouts
    Secret shoppers
    Service evaluators

are always treated like royalty. Sometimes customers in stores, restaurants, or theaters are treated quite poorly. Marketing surveys have found that while customers who are well served share their positive experiences with three other people, those who are ignored, insulted, or irritated will complain to at least ten people. Faced with rising competition, businesses that provide services can't afford to lose customers. Increasingly, they are hiring mystery shoppers to make sure that their establishments and employees are working to make clients feel like royalty.

Working undercover, mystery shoppers are a company's eyes and ears. They provide detailed impressions from a shopper's point of view. Most mystery shoppers get jobs from mystery shopping companies. These firms have a variety of clients, ranging from supermarkets and chain clothing stores to movie theaters and amusement parks. When you receive an assignment to have lunch at a restaurant, get your hair done at a salon, or buy toys for your (real or imaginary) toddler, it will generally be in your town and even in your neighborhood. Often, you choose the day and the time you want to go shopping. Expenses such as transportation are usually reimbursed.

As a mystery shopper, you have to act like any other shopper. The difference is that you will be observing every detail of the business you are visiting, albeit very discreetly. You'll also need to take notes in your head, with a pen and paper, or maybe even with a camera (this is known as enhanced shopping). Among your goals is to observe whether employees are doing their jobs efficiently and treating customers well. Are salespeople friendly and knowledgeable about the products they are selling? Do cashiers give proper change and receipts? You'll also determine whether the business in question meets with all safety, security, and hygienic standards. Are bathrooms clean and stocked with toilet paper? Is the lighting bright enough? Is produce old or damaged? Is the fire escape blocked? Was that a cockroach running across the floor? Not only will your observations help businesses improve their services, but they can also alert owners to serious problems that could otherwise result in accidents, expensive fines, or damaging lawsuits.

Mystery shoppers will sometimes make purchases. While you usually can't keep the clothes, you can eat the food at a restaurant, sample the rides at an amusement park, and watch the movie at a theater (often with popcorn). Other times, however, you simply evaluate a service. Some people are even hired to visit Web sites and go shopping online. Once your shopping session is over,

Mystery shoppers need to make many observations when going through the checkout at a supermarket or store. They must take into account everything from the cashier's efficiency and friendliness to whether correct change is given and how clean the conveyor belt is kept.

you have to fill out a detailed form with your observations. Being a clear and precise writer is important. Although mystery shoppers are usually hired to give a company feedback on its own products and services, in some cases you'll be hired to shop a business's main competition.

Who Relies on Mystery Shoppers?

Banks
Car dealers and rental companies
Convenience stores and supermarkets
Department stores and clothing chains
Gas stations
Government-run businesses and services
Hair salons
Health clubs
Hotels and motels
Movie theaters and amusement parks
Restaurants

Education and Training

No particular education or training is needed to become a mystery shopper. However, there are various seminars and workshops you can take. You can also consult guide books for tips on breaking into the business and lists of the most reputable mystery shopping companies. The National Center for Professional Mystery Shoppers & Merchandisers is a good source for information. This organization offers the KASST (Knowledge and Skill Set Test). After you take the exam, you can call yourself a certified mystery shopper.

Salary

In general, payment depends on the type of shopping you do and the number of hours you work. Sometimes, you'll also receive an allowance for purchases and a reimbursement for your expenses. If you're working under contract for a mystery shopping company, you can expect to earn about $100 a month in cash, food, and merchandise if you shop once a week (an average of two to four hours of work in a month). If you become contracted by more companies, you can shop and earn much more. Many mystery shoppers, particularly students, homemakers, and retired people, are content to work part-time. However, if you are ambitious, organized, and succeed in getting yourself contracted by fifteen or twenty top mystery shopping companies (there are hundreds of companies, but exercise some caution since many are hoaxes), you can earn as much as $20,000 to $25,000 a year. You might even want to consider opening up your own mystery shopping company with your own list of clients and team of mystery shoppers.

Outlook

Mystery shopping is a new and rapidly growing business. Since companies can't send the same people to shop at the same places, mystery shopping companies are in constant need of new shoppers.

FOR MORE INFORMATION

ORGANIZATIONS

Mystery Shopping Providers Association (MSPA)
12300 Ford Road, Suite 135
Dallas, TX 75234
(972) 406-1104
Web site: http://www.mysteryshop.org
> The MSPA is a worldwide professional trade association dedicated to improving service quality by using anonymous shoppers.

The National Center for Professional Mystery Shoppers & Merchandisers
P.O. Box 311573
Tampa, FL 33680
Web site: http://www.justshop.org
> This nonprofit organization offers training and certification for mystery shoppers and mystery shopping companies. Its Web site has some useful FAQs, references, and links.

National Shopping Service (NSS)
2510 Warren Drive
Rocklin, CA 95677
(800) 800-2704
Web site: http://www.nationalshoppingservice.com
> With thirty-three years of experience, NSS has developed into one of the world's leading mystery shopping providers.

WEB SITES

International Mystery Shopping Alliance
http://www.imsa.org

This union of mystery shopping companies throughout the world offers information about local and international projects. The companies listed here provide shopping opportunities for over half a million mystery shoppers.

BOOKS

Gow, Kailin. *Career KNOWtes: Mystery Shopping* (How to Have Fun and Make Money in a Career You Love). 2nd ed. Irving, TX: Sparklesoup Studios, 2003.
A career guide that explains how to get started and succeed as a mystery shopper.

Newhouse, Ilisha. *Mystery Shopping Made Simple*. New York, NY: McGraw-Hill, 2004.
A step-by-step guide on how to break into the mystery shopping business and get the assignments you want.

Obarski, Anne M. *Surprising Secrets of Mystery Shoppers*. Tarentum, PA: Word Association Publishing, 2003.
Retail snoop Obarski offers an interesting behind-the-scenes look at North American corporations and alerts mystery shoppers to the small details that can make or break a business.

Poynter, James. *Mystery Shopping: Get Paid to Shop*. 4th ed. Denver, CO: Leromi Publishing, 2002.
How to start off, get assignments, and make good money as a mystery shopper. Includes a list of companies to contact for job opportunities.

Stucker, Cathy. *Mystery Shopper's Manual*. 6th ed. Sugar Land, TX: Special Interests Publishing, 2004.
A practical guide—with a lack of "get rich quick" hype—for both beginners and seasoned shoppers.

Weis, Julie, and Lynette Janac. *How to Start and Run Your Own Mystery Shopping Company*. Aventura, FL: Basic Success, 2000.
A training manual that teaches you how to start your own mystery shopping business and work part-time or full-time out of your home.

9

WINE MERCHANT

Imagine traveling around the world, visiting vineyards and tasting the most delicious, often rarest, wines on the planet. Now imagine making a living in such a manner. This is how wine merchants spend much of their time. Of course, after making their purchases, they have to return home and consider how to make money by sharing their discoveries

Autumn is harvest time in the Bordeaux wine-growing region of south-west France. To ensure they get every grape, workers carefully handpick the fruit. If the previous winter has been mild, the summer hot, and it hasn't rained too much, the grapes will make wine that is exceptionally smooth and flavorful, allowing vintners and wine dealers to sell many bottles of Bordeaux at top prices.

with the drinking public that frequents their shops, stores, and restaurants.

Job Description

A wine merchant is a buyer who is an expert at purchasing wines. You can learn about wine by reading books and magazines, but there is no substitute for using your senses.

Buying for Millions

David Andrew grew up in Scotland, where men drink mostly whiskey, not wine. However, when he was ten, his parents let him have his first taste of fine wine and he was smitten. More than twenty years later, Andrew has worked his way up to top wine buyer for America's warehouse supermarket giant Costco.

Surprising as it might seem, Costco is actually the largest wine retailer in North America, with annual sales of $600 million in 2002. And its high revenues aren't due to marketing low-end wines that sell for $3.99 a bottle. Thanks to Andrew's smart purchasing practices, Costco's clients can pick up anything from a delicious $10 bottle of Chilean red to a precious 1998 bottle of Chateau Mouton Rothschild for $165. In fact, an important part of Andrew's job is to journey all over the world seeking out bargains and undiscovered treasures. An example is Chateau Salitis, a French red known as a boutique wine because only 5,000 cases are made each year (Andrew buys almost all of them for Costco). During his travels, he is wined and dined by vintners and ends up tasting over 5,000 wines. If this seems like an awful lot to drink, remember that to keep their tasting abilities sharp and to avoid getting tipsy, professional tasters spit out the wine instead of swallowing it.

Source: Fonda, Daren. "Chateau Margaux Meets Costco." Time, October 20, 2002. Retrieved July 2005 (http://www.time.com/time/globalbusiness/ article/0,9171,1101021028-366290,00.html).

Learning to judge a wine by its scent and, more important, its taste are key skills. Most wine merchants develop these skills by going to organized tastings and traveling to the vineyards where the wines are produced. Discovering an unknown wine from a new region can be just as exciting as savoring a centuries-old classic vintage. Visiting producers allows you to see firsthand all the factors that go into making a good wine, from soil and sunlight to harvest and storage techniques. It is also essential to forge good personal relationships with vintners so you can negotiate pricing and shipping details and monitor production standards (the use of high-quality grapes and proper storage methods, for example).

Many wine merchants are also wine retailers who own or run their own specialty wine shops. Through foreign producers and distributors, local importers and wholesalers, and the Internet, merchants shop for an assortment of wines that will please their customers. In North America, people are increasingly interested in wine and are drinking it more frequently. Although consumers like to try new wines, those who aren't collectors or connoisseurs often don't know which ones to select. Part of your job as a merchant is to stock a wide variety for different tastes and budgets as well as educate your clients about what choices are available. Advising customers on what wines are suitable for certain types of meals or events is another important task.

As sales have grown across North America, wine has moved onto the shelves of larger retailers. People who buy wines on a large scale for liquor stores, supermarkets, wholesalers, and importers are often referred to as wine buyers or wine managers. Wine buyers have to make sure shelves are always filled with wines that are going to sell well. Aside from researching new wines, placing orders with suppliers, and monitoring transportation and delivery, buyers organize promotions and displays and create marketing materials to educate both workers and customers.

Wine buyers are also employed by airlines, cruise ships, and hotels. Upscale hotels and restaurants with extensive wine cellars often employ a sommelier as well. A sommelier is a wine steward. Sommeliers help create a wine menu based on costs, clientele, and a restaurant's cuisine. Aside from selecting and purchasing wines, sommeliers must train

Leading wine expert Serge Dubs has been a sommelier for thirty years. Initially, he was interested in food, not wine. He dreamed of opening a restaurant in his native Alsace, a region in northeastern France. However, he soon realized that he couldn't create dishes without learning about wines to accompany them. Today, his restaurant, L'Auberge de l'Ill, is reputed for both its wine cellar and its food.

staff to treat wine properly (to open and serve it correctly, for example) and make appropriate suggestions to customers based on the food they are eating and the money they are willing to spend. A knowledgeable sommelier can make a big difference in a restaurant's profits since aperitifs, wine, and an after-dinner port or sherry might represent 20 to 40 percent of a customer's lunch or dinner check.

Education and Training

There are no formal educational requirements for becoming a wine merchant or for working in the wine industry in general. The best thing to do is learn all you can about wine. Many books, magazines, journals, and Web sites are available. Continuing education, hotel and restaurant schools, and culinary institutes offer courses on various aspects of wine tasting and selection. Find out about tastings organized by local wine societies, restaurants, or specialty shops. And if you can, travel to a wine-producing region and learn firsthand about wine by meeting vintners. Any kind of part-time or summer job in the wine industry will help you learn about wine and retail and provide you with useful contacts. Working at a vineyard or wine shop, or as a waiter or bartender's assistant in a hotel or restaurant are all excellent ways to learn about the business.

Salary

Earnings for wine merchants can vary depending on whether you have your own store or work as a buyer for a large retail chain. Starting out you might earn about $20,000 a year. If you are successful and work your way up to a top buyer or managerial position, you could earn as much as $70,000. Although sommeliers who are starting out make a low average of $14,000 a year, after ten years on the job, salaries can rise to between $40,000 and $45,000.

Outlook

Job opportunities in the wine industry are expected to increase as North Americans become more educated about wines, recognize its many health benefits (when drunk in moderation), and take advantage of increased access to wines from all over the world.

FOR MORE INFORMATION

ORGANIZATIONS

The American Sommelier Association
580 Broadway, Suite 716
New York, NY 10012
(212) 226-6805
Web site: http://www.americansommelier.com
> A nonprofit, national organization with local chapters that run classes, tastings, and events revolving around wine education and enjoyment. Also offers courses and certification for sommeliers.

WEB SITES

Wine Business Online
http://www.winebusiness.com/company
> This leading provider of information and services for the wine industry publishes two journals, *Wine Business Monthly* and *Wine Business Insider*, and the Web site Winejobs.com, which lists job openings.

Wine.com
http://www.wine.com

The world's largest online wine store allows you to track down more than 10,000 domestic and imported wines by type, region, price, and winery. Includes ratings and tips from wine experts.

Wine Lovers Page
http://www.wineloverspage.com
One of the Web's largest and most popular wine appreciation sites. Includes wine tips, an online tasting course, encyclopedia, and international wine shop directory.

BOOKS

Johnson, Hugh. *Hugh Johnson's Pocket Wine Book 2006*. London, England: Mitchell Beazley, 2005.
A slim and complete quick-reference guide to wines with reviews of wines and wineries, glossary of grape types, and advice for matching food and wine, written by one of the world's most knowledgeable wine writers.

Kolpan, Steven, Brian H. Smith, and Michael A. Weiss. *Exploring Wine: The Culinary Institute of America's Guide to Wines of the World*. 2nd ed. New York, NY: John Wiley & Sons, 2001.
This attractive coffee table book takes readers on a complete tour of the world's wine regions, discussing how various wines are made and drunk.

Robinson, Andrea Immer. *Andrea Immer Robinson's Wine Buying Guide for Everyone 2006: Featuring More than 700 Top Wines Available in Stores and Restaurants*. New York, NY: Broadway Books, 2005.
One of only nine female master sommeliers in the world, Robinson uses easy-to-understand terms to teach everything about selecting, tasting, and purchasing wines.

Robinson, Jancis. *How to Taste: A Guide to Enjoying Wine*. New York, NY: Simon & Schuster, 2001.
A wine-tasting workbook with practice exercises, written by the certified master of wine who stars on the PBS series *Jancis Robinson's Wine Course*.

Robinson, Jancis, and Hugh Johnson. *World Atlas of Wine*. 5th ed. New York, NY: Barnes & Noble, 2003.
A best-selling guide to wines of the world written by two leading wine experts.
Zraly, Kevin. *Windows on the World: Complete Wine Course*. 2006 ed. New York, NY: Sterling Publishing Co., Inc., 2005.
A lively, accessible book by the founder of the Windows on the World Wine School teaches you everything about wines.

PERIODICALS

Decanter
Broadway House
2-6 Fulham Broadway
London SW6 1AA
England
Web site: http://www.decanter.com
One of the world's most respected wine magazines, this British publication offers international coverage of the wine industry.

Food and Wine
American Express Publishing Corp.
1120 Avenue of the Americas
New York, NY 10036
Web site: http://www.foodandwine.com
A glossy print magazine that marries gourmet food recipes with fine wine offerings and includes articles on cooking and entertaining.

Wine Spectator
M. Shanken Communications, Inc.
387 Park Avenue South
New York, NY 10016
Web site: http://www.winespectator.com/Wine/Home
This print magazine for wine connoisseurs offers reviews, articles, and ratings of wines from all over the world.

10

INTERIOR DECORATOR

Do you enjoy flipping through decorator magazines or housewares catalogs, imagining what would look good in the rooms of your fantasy house? Chances are that, in reality, your rooms are too small and your budget too tiny for the furniture and art you crave. However, as an interior decorator, you can satisfy your yearnings and even make a decent living by buying furniture and decorative objects for other people who do have the space and the budget but lack the time or inclination to decorate themselves.

Job Description

Interior decorators are hired to decorate the insides of homes, offices, hotels, restaurants, bars, and boutiques. As a decorator, you'll rely on your natural flair, eye for detail, sense of color, and experience to decide how to make a space both functional and beautiful. You'll need to be good at making decisions such as what color carpeting a hallway should have, what fabrics should be used for curtains, and what pieces of furniture work well together and how they should be arranged. At the same time, you'll have to know what furnishing resources and products exist as well as where to buy them. Tracking down a rare, eighteenth-century Portuguese antique chair for someone's home or an authentic stagecoach wheel as decoration for a Tex-Mex restaurant can be interesting challenges. So can bargaining for a price that will satisfy your client's budget. Just as important as building up a list of faithful clients is establishing relationships with furniture manufacturers and retailers; antique stores; art galleries; paint, lighting, and hardware stores; and housewares shops. Being on good terms with suppliers allows you to stay up to date about new products and obtain discounts on purchases.

Fabrics can make a room brighter, cozier, or more luxurious. It is important to have a color scheme in mind before deciding on fabrics for curtains, pillows, sofas, and chairs. Practicality is just as important as color. For example, clients with children or pets should stick to thick, easily washable fabrics with patterns and textures that won't wrinkle, wear, or stain.

Since your livelihood as a decorator depends on your clients, you must be sensitive to their needs. Some clients will rely a great deal on your advice. They may not be sure what they want or what decorative options are available for their budget. It is important to find solutions that are as economical and functional as they are attractive.

Taking your clients' desires into account, you'll develop one or more proposals for their approval. Your suggestions will take into account space, lighting, color schemes, paint, fabrics, flooring, doors, and windows, and use of accessories such as rugs, pillows, art objects, and even plants. Once your plans have been approved, you'll go shopping for the agreed-upon furnishings and supplies. Your clients might also want you to recommend painters, carpenters, and other tradespeople as well as to oversee their work. It is therefore important for you to establish connections with good, reliable tradespeople.

A typical school day for a student of interior decoration might include a morning lecture on current trends from a professional decorator, followed by a session on kitchen and bathroom design. In the afternoon, an introduction to color psychology may be followed by an assignment where students put together a sample color scheme for a room.

Many decorators are freelancers who have their own businesses. They get jobs from personal recommendations and marketing of their services via ads and Web sites. Others have full-time jobs with decorating or design firms. Although decorating can be fun, it can also be stressful. Trying to meet deadlines while dealing with fussy clients and unforeseen problems (from no-show workers to decorative "mistakes" such as mismatched colors and

107

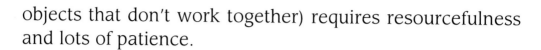

objects that don't work together) requires resourcefulness and lots of patience.

Education and Training

Although no formal training or education is necessary to become an interior decorator, some knowledge of art is useful, as is math for doing measurements and calculations. Decorating courses are available at art schools, community colleges, and continuing-education programs, but you can learn a lot just by consulting decorating and design books and magazines, visiting retailers, window shopping, and checking out interestingly furnished restaurants and hotels. Start downloading or clipping out photographs of design objects and decorator solutions that you admire, and build up your own personal archive of material.

For practice, decorate and redecorate your own room. Then see if your parents, neighbors, or family friends will let you tackle theirs. Make sure to take before and after photographs of your work for a portfolio that you can show future clients. Another good way to learn about decorating and make contacts is to get a part-time job at a decorating firm or retail store specializing in furniture, design objects, and home furnishings and accessories.

Salary

An interior decorator can make anywhere between $20,000 and $40,000 a year. Many decorators work out of their

Decades of Decorating

Betty Sherrill is in her eighties and is chairwoman of McMillen, Inc., America's first professional, full-service interior design firm (founded in 1923). Sherrill herself has been working at McMillen for over fifty years. She has decorated houses for members of the Rockefeller and Kennedy families, as well as the palace of a sheik from Kuwait. She has even decorated the White House (when President Johnson and his family were living there).

Sherrill's first decorating job was the third floor of her family's house in New Orleans when she was still a girl. New wallpaper and a shocking shade of pink in the stairway were the results. In her youth, she also loved combing through antique shops. She recommends that those wanting to enter the field today take decorating courses at art or design school. She also advises that while decorators should keep up with trends, they shouldn't always copy them.

Source: "Designing a Career as an Interior Decorator: Advice from the Experts." CNN.com. September 26, 2000. Retrieved July 2005 (http://archives.cnn.com/2000/STYLE/design/09/26/careers.designing.ap).

Decorators need to understand and work with scale, or size. For instance, the position or angle at which an armchair is placed in a living room can make the chair appear either too small or too dominant and the room seem either empty or cluttered. Meanwhile, a coffee table is too small if it is dwarfed by the chair or sofa beside it, and its surface disappears when covered with a vase and drinks.

homes as part-time freelancers and don't depend exclusively on their earnings as a decorator. An experienced decorator with formal training, a good reputation, and a list of important clients with large budgets can earn $70,000 or more. While some of these high-earning decorators own their own small companies, others work for design or decorating firms or furniture retailers that pay high salaries.

Outlook

According to the U.S. Department of Labor, jobs for interior decorators should increase by more than 20 percent over the next few years. As people become more conscious of design, and as design solutions become increasingly accessible and affordable, both businesses and individuals are seeking out the professional help of decorators to create unique spaces. At the same time, the competitiveness of this field means that good jobs go to those with the most experience and education.

FOR MORE INFORMATION

ORGANIZATIONS

Canadian Decorators' Association (CDECA)
P.O. Box 31037
475 Westney Road North
Ajax, ON L1T 3V2
Canada
(888) 233-2248
Web site: http://www.cdeca.com
Information and resources is provided by Canada's association of professional interior decorators and designers.

Certified Interior Decorators International (CID)
649 SE Central Parkway
Stuart, FL 34994

(772) 287-1855
Web site: http://www.cidinternational.org
  An association that offers education and certification programs
  for professional decorators.

WEB SITES

Canadian Interior Design
http://www.canadianinteriordesign.com
  A site that offers thousands of images related to decorating and
  design and a focus on new ideas and trends.

HGTV (Home & Garden Television)
http://www.hgtv.com/hgtv/dc_furniture/0,1792,HGTV_3437,00.html
  The online version of one of North America's most popular cable
  networks has a great selection of information, links, forums,
  and visuals related to decorating or remodeling every room in
  your house.

Home and Family Network
http://www.homeandfamilynetwork.com/decorating/index.html
  Hundreds of decorating ideas and projects, as well as images of
  home makeovers.

BOOKS

Bradbury, Dominic. *American Designers' Houses*. New York, NY:
  Vendome Press, 2004.
  This attractive coffee-table book takes readers on tours of twenty of
  today's leading interior designers' homes and is accompanied by
  interviews revealing their backgrounds and visions.
Coleman, Brian D. *Extraordinary Interiors: Decorating with Architectural
  Salvage and Antiques*. Layton, UT: Gibbs Smith Publishers, 2005.
  Suggestions on how to decorate cheaply and uniquely by reusing
  and preserving furniture and other elements from old buildings,

businesses, and homes. Such items include 200-year-old doors, vintage sinks, and old office desks.

Goulet, Tag, and Catherine Goulet. *FabJob Guide to Becoming an Interior Decorator*. Seattle, WA: Fabjob.com, 2003.
Available in print or on CD-ROM, this step-by-step introductory guide explains how to get started in the decorating business, touching briefly on a wide variety of topics.

Susanka, Sarah. *Home by Design*. Newtown, CT: Taunton Press, 2004.
Leading architect Susanka explores important design concepts used in well-designed homes.

PERIODICALS

Canadian Interiors
Crailer Communications
360 Dupont Street
Toronto, ON M5R 1V9
Canada
Web site: http://www.canadianinteriors.com
A print and online magazine devoted to interior design with a strong Canadian content.

Dwell
99 Osgood Place
San Francisco, CA 94133
Web site: http://www.dwellmag.com
Print and online versions of this cutting-edge magazine explore new trends and concepts in international architecture and design.

Elle Décor
Hachette Filipacchi Media
1633 Broadway
New York, NY 10019
Web site: http://www.elledecor.com

A stylish print magazine with beautiful photos and articles on home design and living.

Home
Hachette Filipacchi Media
1633 Broadway
New York, NY 10019
Web site: http://www.homemag.com
This magazine offers affordable resources, tips, and solutions for home makeovers, including before and after photos.

House & Garden
Condé Nast Publications
4 Times Square, 17th Floor
New York, NY 10036
Web site: http://www.houseandgarden.com
Upmarket glossy magazine full of attractive photos and all sorts of decorating resources and ideas.

Metropolitan Home
Hachette Filipacchi Media
1633 Broadway
New York, NY 10019
Web site: http://www.neodata.com/hfmus/mhme
Print and online versions of this magazine offer decorative tips and secrets from the world's most renowned designers and decorators.

11

REAL ESTATE AGENT

For most people, buying property is one of the most important decisions, not to mention expenditures, of their lives. If they make a poor decision, buyers can end up losing money and being miserable. However, if they purchase wisely, they will end up with a valuable investment that will greatly enhance their lives. Often the person who makes the difference is a real estate agent. If you would enjoy the satisfaction of helping people locate their ideal residential or commercial space and earning a substantial commission in the process, you might consider a career as a real estate agent.

Job Description

Real estate agents help people find and purchase property. To do this, they must first discover owners who want to sell their property. While many sellers themselves contact real estate firms, agents also spend a lot of time on the phone trying to get listings. Indeed, knowing the market and having many contacts who can give you tips about what might come up for sale are essential. The majority of real estate agents are involved in buying and selling residential properties. They usually start out by getting listings of properties for sale in their own communities or towns, either by word of mouth or by doing research. For example, families that have suffered deaths, divorces, or financial problems often need to sell their homes. Familiarity with a neighborhood is important, since homebuyers consider more than just a house or apartment in itself. Depending on their ages and interests, buyers are also influenced by factors such as security, noise, convenience, and proximity to public transportation, shopping areas, schools, and recreation areas such as parks and bike paths.

It can be difficult for buyers to decide if they like a home when it is filled with the current occupants' furnishings or moving crates, or even when it is completely empty. For this reason, real estate agents often work with the sellers to get them to present their home in the most appealing and sellable way possible.

Most real estate agents are independent contractors who work for a real estate broker. Some brokers are small firms with a few employees, while others are franchises of large national companies such as Century 21 or Royal LePage. In return for finding properties and closing sales between buyers and sellers, the broker pays the agent part of the commission made from the sale. While agents spend a lot of time in the field, brokers manage the office, monitor agents, and tend to the business and administrative details of real estate transactions.

As an agent, your goal is to get sellers to list their properties with you. When people want to buy a home, they'll contact you and ask to see your listings. After meeting with clients to determine what type of space they're looking for and how much they can spend, you'll select promising properties from your list and set up a time to show them to your clients. Often, visits will take place in the evening or on weekends, when people have more free time. Being sensitive to your clients' needs and what exactly they're looking for are essential traits for a successful agent. Moreover, when buyers have questions—How old is the furnace? What are the local zoning laws? How much are property taxes? Is the property in a flood zone?—it is your job to find out the answers.

If the buyers are interested in a certain property, you want to do everything you can to help them obtain a good deal. If the asking price is steep, you can help negotiate with the seller or recommend banks and mortgage companies where the buyer can get financing. As an agent, you act as a mediator between buyers and sellers. Buyers might also ask you to negotiate certain renovations or recommend a house inspector to make sure the house is in good condition. Once both sides have agreed on a price and details of the transfer, you are responsible for drawing up a contract. After the contract has been signed and the sale is finalized, everybody should end up a winner: buyers will have their new home, sellers will have their money, and you will have the satisfaction of a job well done along with your commission.

Real estate agents usually try to take buyers to see a house during a time of day when all the home's features, both internal and external, appear at their best. Factors such as the amount and quality of light a house and its surrounding property receive can be important considerations for many buyers.

Some agents buy and sell commercial property. Commercial property includes office and retail space, hotels and restaurants, factories, warehouses, and land to be developed, as well as industrial and agricultural real estate. Commercial real estate agents usually work for large or specialized companies and focus on one type of commercial real estate—office space, for example. For this type of real estate, it is essential to have a considerable amount of knowledge concerning the type of property you are dealing with as well as the specific business needs of your clients. For instance, if you are selling a factory, you'll need to inform your buyer about factors such as the region's transportation systems, utilities, and labor supply.

Education and Training

The background that most real estate agents share is a high school diploma and solid communication skills. An increasing number of people, however, are taking real estate courses at community or junior colleges. Local associations affiliated with the National Association of Realtors also offer courses on various aspects of real estate. However, the best way to train for a real estate career is by acquiring on-the-job experience. Try to get an assistant's job or internship with a firm in your neighborhood. You'll usually start off helping agents or brokers by answering phones and trying to get property listings.

Before you can call yourself a real estate agent, you have to be eighteen years old and must obtain a license. Each state and province has its own set of requirements, including practical experience, course work, and one or more exams. Often, larger brokers offer their own training sessions and preparatory classes.

Salary

Most real estate agents earn commissions rather than salaries. Commissions are a percentage of the price buyers pay for property. The longer you work and the more successful you are, the higher the commissions you will make. Because they have no clients and little experience, agents who are starting out make almost no money in the first year. It could take weeks or months to get your first sale. Over time, however, you can make between $20,000 and $50,000 a year. The top 10 percent of agents make over $80,000. It is the possibility of making such high earnings that motivates many agents.

Outlook

As population and real estate development in North America continue to grow, people will be moving more and buying and selling more property. Real estate is also increasingly viewed as a sound financial investment. Many people buy property that they then rent out or renovate and resell for a profit. All of these factors will mean more opportunities for real estate agents. Technology, however, will also allow a single agent to do the work formerly done by several. Instead of traveling to visit properties, agents and clients can view exteriors and interiors on the Internet. Cell phones and computers minimize the time spent on transactions and even allow many agents to work at home instead of at brokers' offices.

FOR MORE INFORMATION

ORGANIZATIONS

National Association of Exclusive Buyer Agents
541 South Orlando Avenue, Suite 300
Maitland, FL 32751
(800) 986-2322
Web site: http://www.naeba.org
> Buyer agents work exclusively with buyers (instead of sellers) to help them locate, finance, inspect, and purchase the ideal property. This association's Web site offers lists of exclusive buyer agents.

National Association of Realtors
430 North Michigan Avenue
Chicago, IL 60611-4087
(800) 874-6500
Web site: http://www.realtor.org
> The United States' leading organization for realtors offers a wealth of information concerning every aspect of national and international real estate. The Web site includes news reports, industry research, and information about ethics, education, and events.

Real Estate Institute of Canada
5407 Eglinton Avenue West, Suite 208
Toronto, ON M9C 5K6
Canada
(416) 695-9000
Web site: http://www.reic.ca
> This association educates and certifies Canadian real estate professionals and creates networking opportunities between agents and brokers.

Society of Industrial and Office Realtors
1201 New York Avenue NW, Suite 350
Washington, DC 20005
(202) 449-8200
Web site: http://www.sior.com
   This leading commercial and industrial real estate association provides professional services, publications, and educational courses.

WEB SITES

Real-Estate-Agents.com
http://real-estate-agents.com
   A comprehensive directory of links to real estate agents throughout Canada and the United States.

Realty Times
http://realtytimes.com
   Buying and selling advice, money-making tips, and industry reports from expert columnists make this online news site a leading reference for real estate agents.

BOOKS

Cook, Frank. *21 Things I Wish My Broker Had Told Me: Practical Advice for New Real Estate Professionals.* Chicago, IL: Dearborn Real Estate Education, 2002.
   This book of practical advice written for real estate agents features real-life stories, some of them quite humorous, from successful professionals.
Edwards, Kenneth W. *Your Successful Real Estate Career.* 4th ed. New York, NY: American Management Association, 2003.
   A comprehensive guide for anyone looking into a career in real estate, this book deals with everything from getting a license to succeeding in a highly competitive business.

Kennedy, Danielle, and Warren Jamison. *How to List and Sell Real Estate in the 21st Century*. Upper Saddle River, NJ: Pearson, 1999. Kennedy is a successful broker and professional speaker who shares techniques for embarking upon a career in real estate along with tips and real-life anecdotes.

McCrea, Bridget. *The Real Estate Agent's Field Guide: Essential Insider Advice for Surviving in a Competitive Market*. New York, NY: American Management Association, 2004. A basic overview of the real estate industry.

Sullivan, Marilyn. *The Complete Idiot's Guide to Success as a Real Estate Agent*. Indianapolis, IN: Alpha Books, 2003. This book offers step-by-step advice for people who want to get into the real estate business. Includes examples of seller and buyer transactions and tips on how to conduct an open house.

PERIODICALS

Realtor
National Association of Realtors
430 North Michigan Avenue
Chicago, IL 60611-4087
Web site: http://www.realtor.org
This print and online magazine from North America's leading real estate association contains articles, interviews, and business tips and techniques. The online version features exclusive reviews, columns, and resources.

ARTICLES

Obringer, Lee Ann. "How Buying a House Works." HowStuffWorks. Retrieved June 2005 (http://money.howstuffworks.com/house-buying.htm).

12

STOCKBROKER

Perhaps no job is as thrilling or as stressful as being a stockbroker. Buying company stock in order to earn money for clients is like getting paid to gamble. It can be exciting, not to mention extremely profitable, if you are a savvy and quick-thinking buyer. It can be disastrous if you aren't. If you love the idea of a career that is a

Above, stockbrokers and traders work on the trading floor at the New York offices of JPMorgan, a major brokerage firm. With the rise of electronic trading over the Internet, brokers are selling fewer stocks but more software that helps clients to invest by themselves. Those entering the field have to be technologically savvy so they can advise clients on using these programs that allow them to buy and sell on their own.

roller-coaster ride, with ups and downs but never a dull moment, you'd make a good candidate for a stockbroker.

Job Description

Stockbrokers buy stocks for individuals and corporations who have money to invest and want to make a profit. In order to buy or sell stock, people must go through a registered broker. A broker generally works for a financial institution, bank, or brokerage house that is a member of a stock exchange. You may have heard of major brokerage houses such as Merrill Lynch and Morgan Stanley. The stock exchange is, in effect, a big market where stocks of public corporations are bought and sold by investors from all over the world.

If investors want to buy or sell stock, they will call you up and you'll get in touch with a trader who works on the floor of the stock exchange. After the trader buys or sells the stock, he will notify you, confirming that the transaction was carried out according to regulations. After recording this information, you will inform your clients.

This process sounds simple, but it is actually quite complex. First of all, it takes years to build up a solid list of investor clients. To get clients, you have to be aggressive, confident, and good at networking. You might end up making 100 calls a day! Even experienced brokers spend an enormous amount of time on the phone trying to land new clients. The way to get and keep clients is to impress them with your knowledge of the market. This requires staying up to date with everything that is going on in the domestic and global economy. You'll spend significant parts of your day reading economic papers, financial and industry reports, journals, and indexes; searching the Internet for new investment opportunities; and monitoring your clients' current investments.

Stock Talk

We hear about the stock market on the news every day. However, most people don't really know how the stock market works. Here are some basic explanations.

When a person or a group of people want to start a business, they need **capital** (money). In order to raise capital, they create a public corporation. A **corporation** is an independent entity, a type of "virtual person" with its own social security number that can own property and in whose name deals and contracts can be signed.

After estimating how much their corporation needs, the owners issue **shares**. When investors—either individuals or companies—purchase shares, they are investing money in the company and becoming partial owners. The corporation can use this money to buy property, equipment, and materials, and pay salaries, all with the aim of growing as a business and earning a **profit**.

Profits can be reinvested in the company to create more growth or paid out as **dividends** to shareholders. Ultimately, stock represents ownership of a company's assets and profits. Shareholders elect a board of directors to run the corporation efficiently and profitably.

Shares of stock are sold on **stock exchanges**. Canada's main stock exchange is the Toronto Stock Exchange (TSX), located on Bay Street. The three major stock exchanges in the United States are the American Stock Exchange (AMEX), the National Association of Securities Dealers Automated Quotations (NASDAQ), and the New York Stock Exchange (NYSE). The NYSE, located on lower Manhattan's Wall Street, handles stock for close to 3,000 companies. Its total stock is worth more than 20 trillion dollars, making it the largest trading market in the world.

In 1996, a high-tech wireless data system was introduced at the New York Stock Exchange (NYSE) to increase the speed of buying and selling transactions on the floor. More and more, all levels of stock market trading rely on the use of high-tech computers and software programs.

If stock prices are going to go up or down, you have to phone your client fast and together decide how much to buy or sell. This has to be done very quickly, since prices can rise and fall suddenly. Being responsible for your clients' investments—often their money is for children's college funds or their own retirement plans—is an enormous responsibility. Your timing and advice are crucial and can literally affect lives. Some brokers thrive in this exhilarating but stressful high-stakes atmosphere. Others can't take it. Many new brokers leave their jobs within their first two years.

Education and Training

Although a college degree isn't necessary, more stockbrokers are going to college. As markets and economies grow more complex, studying subjects such as business, economics, and finance can help give you a solid background. Since stock market transactions are increasingly being done by computer, some computer background is also useful. Probably the best training you can get, however, is on-the-job experience. In the end, knowing how to instill confidence in customers is the most important skill for a successful broker.

When you first start out working for a brokerage firm, you will receive in-house training. This may last anywhere from four months to two years. Since all brokers need to be registered, most firms will also help you prepare for the

Hand signals constitute a sign language that allows traders at an exchange to quickly communicate basic information. Verbal communication often cannot be heard on the noisy floor, especially across wide distances. Signals let traders and other floor employees exchange data such as how much a certain stock is worth at any given moment and how many shares a client might want to purchase.

General Securities Registered Representative Exam, administered by the National Association of Securities Dealers (NASD). Depending on your state of residence, you may also need to pass the Uniform Securities Agents State Law Examination, which gives you a license to be a stockbroker. In Canada, registration and qualification are monitored by the Investment Dealers Association of Canada (IDA).

Salary

When you start out as a broker, before you have any clients of your own, you will probably receive a small base salary—around $20,000 to $25,000—from the firm that hired you. However, once you start establishing your own list of clients, you will also begin earning commissions. A commission is a percentage of the value of your client's transactions. This means that the more clients you have, and the more you can convince them to buy or sell, the more commissions you will make. Because of this, most brokers are highly motivated to sell—their efforts can literally make them millionaires.

In truth, however, very few brokers become millionaires. The average American broker earns a comfortable $60,000 a year. But those Wall Street and Bay Street players who have a knack for working hard and selling hard can easily earn between $100,000 and $150,000; sometimes they earn much more. Of course, earnings depend enormously on the state of the economy and the market. During rough times, even top brokers can see their commissions disappear as investors stop buying.

Outlook

As people's incomes increase, they will seek more investment opportunities. There will be particular growth with respect to individuals making investments for their retirement. Also, as the market becomes increasingly global, new opportunities will open up. At the same time, however, with buying and selling stocks over the Internet becoming more common, brokers can take on more clients, making it tougher for newcomers to break into the field.

Beginning brokers always have a tough time. Starting out, without a client list, can be difficult and very competitive. Competition is especially intense in large firms, particularly those in New York, where there are often more applicants than jobs.

FOR MORE INFORMATION

ORGANIZATIONS

The Canadian Securities Administrators (CSA)
Tour de la Bourse
800, Square Victoria, Suite 4130
Montreal, QC H4Z 1J2
Canada
(514) 864-9510
Web site: http://www.csa-acvm.ca
    The CSA coordinates regulation of the Canadian capital markets
    with the aim of protecting market investors from improper practices.

Investment Dealers Association of Canada
(Toronto Headquarters)
121 King Street West, Suite 1600
Toronto, ON M5H 3T9
Canada
(416) 364-6133

Web site: http://www.ida.ca
> The representative association of Canada's securities industry regulates trading and traders throughout the country. It is also responsible for licensing brokers and protecting the public from abuses.

National Association of Securities Dealers, Inc. (NASD)
New York District Office
One Liberty Plaza
New York, NY 10006
(212) 858-4000
Web site: http://www.nasdr.com
> The world's largest private-sector regulator of financial services. By law, all brokerage firms and stockbrokers must register and write qualifying exams with the NASD and comply with its rules regarding ethical trading.

Securities Industry Association
New York Office
120 Broadway, 35th Floor
New York, NY 10271
(212) 608-1500
Web site: http://www.sia.com
> An association of investment bankers, brokers, dealers, and mutual fund companies concerned with building public trust and confidence in trading markets. Offers training and education for members, and information and services to the public.

U.S. Securities and Exchange Commission (SEC)
100 F Street NE
Washington, DC 20549
(202) 551-6551
Web site: http://www.sec.gov

The SEC protects investors against misinformation and fraud. It makes and enforces laws and rules that govern the securities industry in the United States to ensure investors receive all the information they need to make sound investments.

WEB SITES

BrokerHunter.com
http://www.brokerhunter.com
> A site designed to bring together brokerage firms and job-seeking sales assistants and brokers.

NASDAQ Stock Market
http://www.nasdaq.com
> NASDAQ is the largest U.S. electronic stock market, listing over 3,000 companies. Its site offers up-to-date market quotes and information about companies and domestic and global markets.

New York Stock Exchange (NYSE)
http://www.nyse.com
> NYSE provides real-time quotes, market information for brokers and individual investors, trading regulations, and news from the world's leading stock market.

Toronto Stock Exchange
http://www.tsx.com
> Up-to-date information on Canadian stocks and companies is supplied by the nation's main stock exchange. Includes a list of employment opportunities.

BOOKS

Anuff, Joey, and Gary Wolf. *Dumb Money: Adventures of a Day Trader*. New York, NY: Random House, 2000.

This book offers a first-person account of the fast-paced world of day trading with its many highs and pitfalls.

Boik, John. *Lessons from the Greatest Stock Traders of All Time: Proven Strategies Active Traders Can Use Today to Beat the Market*. New York, NY: McGraw-Hill, 2004.
Useful trading tips and strategies from some of America's most successful traders.

Dorsey, Thomas J. *Thriving as a Broker in the 21st Century*. Princeton, NJ: Bloomberg Press, 1999.
Market watcher Dorsey gives tips for success in the increasingly competitive, globalized, and high-tech world of trading. Includes interviews with some of America's most reputed brokers.

Lefevre, Edwin. *Reminiscences of a Stock Operator*. New York, NY: John Wiley & Sons, 1994. (First published in 1923 by George H. Doran.)
Despite being written in the 1920s, this novel—based on the life of one of America's most famous traders, Jesse Livermore—is still one of the most useful and popular books ever written on the subject of trading and speculation.

PERIODICALS

Barron's
200 Burnett Road
Chicopee, MA 01020
Web site: http://www.barronsmag.com
Barron's is America's leading financial weekly paper, with in-depth news reports and analysis on global financial markets, plus statistics on trading and financial activities.

Wall Street Journal
200 Liberty Street
New York, NY 10281
Web site: http://www.public.wsj.com/home.html
Published six days a week, the *Wall Street Journal* is one of the world's most widely read and respected sources of business news and analysis.

GLOSSARY

aperitif An alcoholic drink served before a meal.

appraisal An authorized examination of an object or piece of property by an experienced specialist in order to assess value.

art deco A decorative and architectural style of the period 1925 to 1940, characterized by geometric designs.

baroque A highly ornamental decorative style in art and architecture, prevalent in Europe between the early seventeenth and mid-eighteenth centuries, characterized by dramatic, curving forms.

commission A fee or percentage of proceeds paid to a broker or agent for his or her services.

commodity A product that is bought and resold.

connoisseur A person with expert knowledge or fine taste.

consignment A form of buying in which the dealer pays the owner after the goods have been sold.

contractor A person who agrees to supply certain materials or do certain work, usually for a predetermined sum.

dilemma A situation in which one has to choose between two difficult options.

discreetly With restraint or care.

enhance To improve in cost, value, or attractiveness.

favoritism Partiality toward a particular person or group.

flair A natural talent or ability.

franchise An agreement in which a company allows another party to use its brand name and to sell or rent its products or services.

guru A trusted guide or adviser.

impressionism A style of painting that originated in France in the 1860s, characterized by painters' use of pure color and small paintbrush strokes to provide visual impressions of the changing effects of light.

layout The overall design of a page, spread, or book.

mediator Someone who works to reach an agreement between people or parties.

New York school A group of painters and poets who worked in New York in the 1950s and were influenced by abstract art.

portfolio A flat, portable case for holding material, such as photographs or drawings, as well as the representative work a person keeps in it.

smitten Infatuated; struck with a favorable impression.

surplus A quantity or amount in excess of what is needed.

vintage Wine, usually of high quality, identified by year and its vineyard or region of origin.

vintner A wine maker or seller.

wholesaler A person or firm that sells goods in large quantities and usually at lower prices than retail.

INDEX

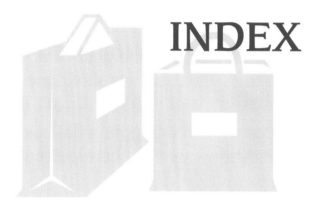

About the Author

Edson Santos is of Brazilian origin and grew up in Rio de Janeiro and Miami. While acquiring a bachelor's degree in literature from New York University, Edson supported himself with many buying-related jobs, some of which—such as mystery shopper and professional shopper—are listed in this book. This is his first book for Rosen Publishing.

Photo Credits

Cover © Philippe Eranian/Corbis; pp. 10, 12 © Ted Streshinsky/Corbis; p. 16 © Steve Marcus/Reuters/Corbis; pp. 21, 26 © Warner Bros. Pictures/Zuma/Corbis; p. 22 © AP/Wide World Photos/Pat Roque; pp. 31, 37 © AP/Wide World Photos/Mary Godleski; p. 32 © Tim Chapman/Getty Images; p. 35 © AP/Wide World Photos/Charlie Riedel; p. 44 © Reuters/Corbis; pp. 42, 46 © Mario Tama/Getty Images; p. 48 © AP/Wide World Photos/Don Ryan; p. 54 © Photo B.D.V./Corbis; pp. 53, 59 © AP/Wide World Photos/Amy Sancetta; p. 56 © AP/Wide World/Norman Dettlaff, the Daily Times; pp. 64, 69 © Sie Productioons/Zefa/Corbis; p. 66 © Harry Sieplinga/HMS Images/The Image Bank/Getty Images; p. 67 © Clay Perry/Corbis; pp. 74, 78 © Steve Liss/Time Life Pictures/Getty Images; p. 76 © Reuters/Corbis; pp. 85, 86 © Phil Cantor/SuperStock, Inc.; p. 89 © Francisco Cruz/SuperStock, Inc.; pp. 94, 95 © AP/Wide World Photos/Bob Edme; pp. 99, 125, 131 © Charles O'Rear/Corbis; pp. 104, 106 © Chris Caroll/Corbis; p. 107 © Bill Bachmann/Index Stock Imagery; p. 110 © Steven S. Miric/SuperStock, Inc.; pp. 115, 117 © AP/Wide World/Damian Dovarganes; p. 119 © Rolf Bruderer/Corbis; p. 126 © Ed Kashi/Corbis; p. 129 © H. Wedewardt/Corbis.

Designer: Evelyn Horovicz; Editor: Elizabeth Gavril